# The Mercy Effect

## A SPIRITUAL GUIDE FOR MANAGING CONFLICT

# GARY PETTY

Little Frog PUBLISHING

All biblical citations come from the *New King James Version* (NKJV),
Holman Bible Publishers, Nashville, Tennessee © 2013; and
the *New International Version* (NIV), Zondervan Bible Publishers,
Grand Rapids Michigan, © 1978.

Little Frog Publishing
Round Rock, Texas
www.littlefrogpublishing.com

ISBN 978-0-9994251-1-4 (Paperback Edition)

Printed in the United States of America

# CONTENTS

# Preface: Why Write this Book?

This is a book about principles I have not yet mastered.

This may seem like a strange confession since books are usually written by people who have become experts in their respective fields and share their expertise with their readers. But authentic Christianity isn't a "you have finally arrived" experience. The conviction to be a true disciple of Jesus Christ is a daily adventure of ever learning and ever changing by applying the teachings of the Master.

This is a book about conflict. I will identify the causes of hostility, bickering and antagonism that define so many relationships. We will also look at the difficult reality that in order to deal with the struggles we have with our spouses, co-workers and members of our congregations, we must first explore our personal conflict with God. This conflict with God, and how he reconciles us to him, is the source of the help and understanding that leads us to emotional healing and the ability to forgive.

The Bible reveals that only when we deal with the internal issues of conflict can we begin to manage the actual relationship issues. I use the term "manage" because it is not always possible to resolve conflict. Emotional and spiritual maturity, and happiness, requires that we learn to accept that not all conflict will be resolved to our satisfaction. There are separate chapters on how to manage conflict as the injured person and as the offender. In the end we discover the profound meaning of Christ's statement, "Blessed are the peacemakers, for they shall be called the sons of God." Like all personal searching for truth and healing, I found nothing new, but trod the path others already discovered. Many of the principles in this book are explained by Viktor Frankl in *Man's Search for Meaning*, Ken Sande's *The Peacemaker*, Dennis Prager's *Happiness is a Serious Problem*, Stephen Covey's *The Seven Habits of Highly Effective People*, Kenneth C. Haugk's *Antagonist in the Church*, Stephen M.R. Covey's *The Speed of Trust*, Dr. David Stoop's *You Are What You Think* and *Forgiving What You'll Never Forget*, as well as many other well-known or obscure authors. Most of all, I found the answers in the Bible, the Creator's instruction book for humanity.

I would like to thank Dan Dowd, Jorge De Campos and my brother-in-law Keith Wilson for their suggestions and edits. There is no way this project would have been completed without the support of my editor Bill Palmer and input from my wife Kim.

This is part of my journey. I pray it helps you on yours.

# 1

# Why Can't We Just Get Along?

We live in a storm of conflict among family members, co-workers and neighbors. The daily news reminds us that Congress is deadlocked in a hot debate about raising taxes while local garbage collectors threaten to go on strike. We come home nervous and in despair because of confrontations at work only to end up in arguments with our spouses. The television newsbreak interrupts our program with another story of a suicide bomber who violently snuffed out the lives of people he didn't even know. Christians, who claim to follow the teachings of the "Prince of Peace," seem as susceptible to destructive conflict as secular society.

How many husbands and wives, lifelong friends or members of a congregation have abandoned their ideals concerning divorce, friendship or church unity because of unresolved conflicts that ate away at relationships like cancer? Everyone could see the symptoms, but no one could find the cure.

When we remain embroiled in dysfunctional, unresolved conflict, we become increasingly self-absorbed into a sense of hurt or violation until it is almost impossible to sort through the conundrum of negative feelings and thoughts. At this point, it is tough to arrive at any real solutions.

We can either learn to deal with conflicts in healthy ways that build happy, productive relationships leading to co-operation, or we can end up trapped in self-defeating negative feelings. How many people do you know who are filled with indefinable anger and bitterness while defining themselves as victims? In the Sermon on the Mount Jesus said, "Blessed are the peacemakers, for they shall be called sons of God" (Matthew 5:9).

When disagreements in Christian marriages, friendships and business relationships, or differences between members of a congregation, are handled in a spirit of competition and lack of forgiveness, Christians experience the same destructive outcomes as secular society. Clearly there is something seriously wrong with how we understand and apply the teachings of Jesus Christ. Christians can't model peacemaking to society if we don't understand and practice peacemaking among ourselves.

How can you become a peacemaker in an increasingly conflicted, polarized and violent world? What is the difference between peacemaking and appeasement? How can we deal with the emotions of being mistreated or betrayed? These are difficult spiritual issues and real solutions involve more than just applying some rules of conflict resolution and sharpening communication skills.

The answers to these questions are discovered in a journey of personal evaluation in what the Bible calls "the ministry of reconciliation." This journey begins with being personally reconciled to God and leads to learning how to reconcile with family members, neighbors, co-workers and members of your congregation. It is a necessary journey if we want to be "called the sons of God."

Let's begin our journey by looking at five basic human needs and desires that motivate destructive conflicts. We'll be returning to these points later to explore how the Bible teaches us to deal with these core issues.

## The Need to be Healed Emotionally

Kurt was a man coming undone. He sat alone in a room full of people busy with activity. Laughter and conversation swirled around him, but Kurt had a scowl on his face and anguish in his eyes. He explained to me that he had been lied to by Jim, a trusted authority figure. The wound was so deep that Kurt was sure he could no longer trust anyone.

Kurt's anger was compounded by the fact that not long after the offense Jim died, leaving Kurt with no way to seek justice or to receive the apology he needed. The hurt was all consuming. "It is as if," Kurt explained, "he reaches up out of the grave and controls my life."

Although the names have been changed, this story is based on real people. Are you like Kurt, filled with anguish, waiting for an offender to help you heal by admitting wrong?

Often, we describe emotional hurts in physical terms like "open wounds" and "deep scars." We become convinced that the pain will go away only when the other person receives justice or admits the wrong. But what happens when a person refuses to admit the wrong or justice seems to be ignored? At that point we can become trapped in a never-ending state of turmoil without any hope of resolution. All aspects of life become increasingly bitter, robbing us of peace and happiness. The need to have others heal our emotional hurts is a major reason we have so much trouble resolving conflicts with people who have offended us.

## Expectations that other People Will Satisfy All of Our Needs and Desires

All of us desire to be happy, to please our senses and to avoid both physical and emotional pain. These desires aren't always wrong. God designed us to need and desire love and friendship, to enjoy the proper use of our senses, and to avoid stresses that make us physically and emotionally sick.

We naturally approach all relationships with expectations. When people don't fulfill those expectations, we end up feeling disappointed, which can lead to conflict. The source of many marital battles is the feeling of deprivation. A husband and wife may feel deprived of emotional support or sexual fulfillment. Similarly, many office clashes stem from unfulfilled expectations for promotion or monetary rewards.

Problems arise when others don't meet our expectations. When we perceive that others are blocking our happiness or pleasure, or when we see these individuals as a source of pain, then we put on emotional battle armor and prepare for hand-to-hand conflict.

The Bible teaches that the first humans had a peaceful relationship with God, but they chose their own standards of right and wrong. It says that the tree of the knowledge of good and evil appeared "good for food, pleasant to the eyes, and a tree desirable to make one wise" (Genesis 3:6).

These motivations aren't evil in themselves. It is not necessarily a wrong desire to enjoy good food, nor is wanting to please the senses or to seek wisdom necessarily wrong. The problem is when we go against God's instructions, deciding for ourselves how we will satisfy our needs and desires. We seek gratification in ways that are rebellious toward God and harmful to us and to other people.

The apostle James wrote: "Where do wars and fights come from among you? Do they not come from your desires for pleasure that war in your members?" (James 4:1).

One of the surest paths to unhappiness and constant frustration is to become obsessed with our own wants and needs. Selfishness is a root of dysfunctional conflict. Selfish motivations can feel so right, even when the resulting behaviors are destructive to our relationships and personal well-being.

Balancing the desire to fulfill our expectations with the

reality of relating to and loving others is one of the challenges to emotional well-being.

## The Need for Control

The natural human reaction to conflict is fight-or-flight. These are normal reactions when we face physical threats, but we also respond with fight-or-flight behavior when confronted with non-physical conflict. We either fight to protect our perceived rights, our self-image or our emotional security, or we run away so that we can avoid the uncomfortable work involved in working out problems with others. Both of these reactions to conflict are based in fear.

The hard truth is that much of what happens in life is beyond our control. We had no choice in our parents or the world economy. We do not choose to have neighbors who like loud mufflers on their cars, nor can we control whether our spouses will agree on the color of fabric we prefer on the new couch. In the chaos of life, we are often driven by a need to control situations and people so that we can protect our rights, our self-image and our emotional security. This need can become an obsession.

At the core of our obsession to control everything in our lives is a reality that we are acting as if we are gods. We desire that every person react in a manner we choose, and that every conflict ends as we ordain. At this point, we can become self-idolaters, creating a mental image of ourselves as the final judges of right and wrong in every disagreement we have with others.

## Pride

Ben was a Connecticut merchant in the American colonial period. As his business fortunes rose, so did his resentment of British taxation.

At the outset of the American Revolution, Ben was elected captain of the local militia. He organized them into an effective fighting force and presented a bold plan for seizing the British forts at Crown Point and Ticonderoga. The plan was accepted, and the expedition successful, although the undertaking was marred by the fact that Ben was in conflict with fellow officers. Ben spent a large sum of personal money financing the campaign, which created financial difficulty for his family. Added to his financial hardships was the tragedy of his wife's sudden death.

Eventually Ben caught the attention of George Washington. Washington saw through Ben's bluster and tactlessness, recognizing him as a leader and good tactician. Ben's leadership helped the colonial army survive the hardships and defeat of an ill-fated Canadian expedition.

Returning home, Ben found himself faced with charges of forcing Canadian merchants to give food to his starving army. This was a bitter pill to an already wounded pride. Still, he continued to fight for the Revolution and defeated a British fleet on Lake Champlain.

It was obvious that this successful commander was next in line for promotion to major general. The Continental Congress, under political pressure, felt that military leaders should be selected more evenly from among all the colonies. New England had more than their fair share of major generals. Ben was denied the promotion.

Ben was then seriously wounded in the Second Battle of Saratoga and during his recovery he was given command of the garrison in Philadelphia. Having spent much of his personal fortune in the war effort, he decided to enjoy the fruits of his labors. It wasn't long until British sympathizers used his extravagant lifestyle to bring charges against him.

This was the last straw. He became bitter and disillusioned. At this point Ben—Benedict Arnold—betrayed his country. Mention the name of Benedict Arnold today and nobody remembers his victories and bravery. All people remember is the crime of treason. What causes a person to betray his own ideals? Benedict Arnold felt stabbed in the back by jealous fellow officers. He had charges brought against him by British sympathizers. Congress refused to repay money he had spent out of his pocket for war expenses. Eventually, he convinced himself that the leaders of the Revolution were incompetent. He lost faith in the cause of American liberty.

For a person to betray everything he loves and believes, he must first feel betrayed. Once a person allows bitterness over another person's actions or words to become an emotional obsession, he becomes consumed with a need for vindication. Arnold's disillusionment in the Revolution was rooted in his concern with personal injustices, both real and perceived. Always a prideful man, Arnold's pride became more important than his values.

Pride is an exaggerated view of our importance. Pride is a great deceiver. It makes us forget our spiritual principles and centers our attention on what we feel we deserve because of our effort and sacrifice. It changes our focus from how we treat others to how others treat us. Pride sidetracks the effort needed to deal with important issues, and centers our energies on attacking personalities and the wrong actions of others. Character, the internal force to do right, becomes easily manipulated by a drive to be proved right no matter what the price. When we are driven by pride, conflict is inevitable and the solution is seen as a need to defeat the other person.

While all four of these basic human emotional needs and desires contribute to conflict; there is one core cause for all human dysfunctions, broken relationships and violent behaviors that we need to explore.

## Our Conflict with God

Shakespeare's Hamlet proclaimed: "What a piece of work is a man, how noble in reason, how infinite in faculty, in form and moving how express and admirable, in action like an Angel, in apprehension how like a god..."

Scan the news headlines and you get a different concept of humanity: war, murder, terrorism, despotism, crime and endless conflict. If mankind is "in apprehension how like a god," why can't we solve our problems? Hamlet's cynical view was that humanity isn't really noble because in the end we are just dust.

On one hand, human beings are capable of artistic creativity and brilliance in engineering and mathematics. We experience love, the outgoing concern for others that provides life so much of its richness and meaning. At the same time, humanity is capable of hatred, destruction, prejudice and murder. All too often it seems that people are driven by the darker side of our nature. This is never truer than when we are in angry disagreement with each other.

What is it about human nature that drives us to destructive conflicts?

The ability to reason, to formulate complex decisions and to choose various courses of action makes human beings infinitely different from any other creature on the earth. Hungarian-born Joseph Kovach was only 15 when he was sent to a Russian prison. He spent four years in a bleak and meaningless world. Kovach later said: "When I look at the months, the years, they were empty. There's nothing in terms of thinking, of planning, of remembering the past or planning for the future. It felt almost as though I was hibernating" (*The Mind*, Richard M. Restak, M.D., 1988, p. 271).

Eventually, he was moved to a gulag containing a small library. Reading opened his mind to ideas and creativity. When he was finally released Kovach moved to the United States where he attended the University of Chicago.

Kovach concluded: "Ultimately, it is our mental apparatus, our capacity to think, our capacity to deal with ideas, our capacity to find unities, coherences in variations—that's what makes us human. We have a way of creating worlds for ourselves, in our heads, and sharing those worlds" (Restak, p. 273).

The more complex the life form the more it can "learn." Still, most behaviors of even the highest forms of animals are primarily instinctive. This isn't true of human beings. Brain size and biology can't entirely explain humanity's uniqueness. So what creates the differences? The Bible states that animals were created "after their kind," but human beings were made in the "image of God" (Genesis 1:25-27).

How are you made in the image of God? Let's consider some of the ways human beings are fundamentally different from animals.

- **Self-consciousness and intelligence.** The human mind gives us capacity for reasoned thought. Biological instinct isn't the driving force that determines most of our behaviors.

- **The search for meaning.** Our unique human qualities lead us to search for meaning in our personal lives as well as meaning in human life as a whole. Libraries are full of books by authors searching for purpose in life. Every human culture tries to formulate meaning by producing its own religions, myths and philosophies. We have a need to find meaning and purpose in suffering. Even children want to know why the pet dog died, or why people get sick.

- **Empathy.** This leads us to another unique human trait—the capacity for conscious empathy by sharing in another's suffering.

- **The ability to think and plan in time.** It's an amazing aspect of the human mind to think in terms of past, present and future. We have aspirations to achieve, so we set goals and organize activities in blocks of time. When was the last time you saw a gorilla or chimp open his calendar to make an appointment? The capacity to conceive of time gives us the ability to envision our own deaths. From the funeral pyres of ancient civilizations to the ceremonies of our modern age, we are ever searching for meaning in death and for hope in an afterlife. These activities are foreign to animals.

- **Creativity.** Human beings are unique in their development of art, music and literature.

- **The ability for abstract thought.** An architect can visualize a skyscraper, draw lines on a piece of paper called a blueprint, then give the blueprint to a builder who studies those lines and physically constructs the vision that existed originally only in the mind of the architect. Much human learning is through the five senses, yet the human mind stretches beyond the senses to encompass abstract concepts such as infinity, liberty, beauty and humor.

  Beavers, through instinct, build the same types of dam generation after generation. There isn't a raging river on the globe that human beings, through creative problem solving, can't dam and use to generate electricity. What's different is that our creative abilities allow us to adapt to highly complex situations and to solve new problems.

- **The ability to create languages.** Human beings comprehend connections among large numbers of words. We have the ability to learn different languages, even "animal languages."

- The capacity for scientific thought. This includes experimentation and developing theories.

- The ability to change our environment, our personality, our character, our habits and even our physical looks.

- The ability to experience, communicate and even manage complex emotions, such as joy and peace, and conversely, depression and despair through deliberate thought.

- The ability to conceive of morality. Because human beings can conceive of a choice between inherently right and inherently wrong behavior, we have a capacity for a relationship with God.

Obviously, human beings are finite. We have physical limitations and we are morally flawed.

However, the Bible emphasizes our astounding uniqueness compared with other creations. Every one of us is a distinct person with self-awareness and self-will. We have the ability to reason as well as the capacity for a wealth of emotional experiences, including empathy and love. These attributes give us the capacity to develop relationships with God and with other human beings.

Why do human beings possess such remarkable abilities, which are reflections of the Creator, and still our lives are filled with anger and broken relationships? If we are designed to have a relationship with God why does it seem like God is sort of an absentee landlord in the affairs of the average person?

## The Knowledge of Good and Evil

The answer to the dilemma of human nature is discovered in the first three chapters of Genesis. The first human beings experienced a nurturing, loving relationship with their Creator until they decided to choose for themselves, using their own reasoning and desires, the definitions of right and wrong by eating of the Tree of the Knowledge of Good and Evil. Through this experience, they corrupted their human nature. They became deformed images of God.

Each of us possesses a fundamental nature that is a mixture of good and evil. We may be created in the image of God, but all of us have become terribly flawed images. All destructive conflicts between people are a direct result of the dysfunctional conflict each of us has with our Creator.

The apostle Paul wrote, "...the carnal [natural] mind is enmity against God; for it is not subject to the law of God, nor indeed can be" (Romans 8:7).

At the core of every human being, even the best of us, is a natural hostility toward God and a rejection of his instructions on how to live. We can solve nothing in life until we first deal with our personal conflict with God.

It's easy to experience religious ceremonies as a temporary emotional fix for the spiritual hunger that plagues our deepest longings. We can then avoid facing our original purpose as a being made in the image of God, thereby denying how disfigured we've become. All too often a bland, culturally correct Christianity allows us to continue the destructive mental and emotional processes that leave us spiritually empty and at war with others. True Christianity is more than a profession of faith in Jesus. It is the process of recognizing our corrupted nature, accepting Christ's sacrifice, and submitting to God's guidance in creating a new nature. It is the process of being restored to our original purpose as a child of God.

This is what the New Testament calls "the ministry of reconciliation." This message can unleash God's mercy effect in your life.

# 2

# The Ministry of Reconciliation

In the Genesis creation account we see that God created each animal "according to its kind," but human beings are made in the "image" and "likeness" of God. Creativity, logic, love, abstract thought and complex communication skills are all aspects of the mind of the Creator. These are ways in which we are created in his likeness.

If we're made in the image of God, who reveals himself as loving, kind and merciful, then why are human beings filled with hatred, violence and selfishness? Why are intelligent people capable of writing inspiring music and at the same time able to commit terrible crimes against each other? Why do scientists research the intricate human body to create medicines that heal, and at the same time produce biological weapons that kill? Why does the same human genius launch a rocket to explore outer space as well as a missile to the other side of the earth to destroy a city?

The answers to this dilemma lie in understanding that each of us has become a mixture of good and evil. We are all horribly disfigured images of God. The first humans experienced a loving relationship with their Creator. Not only did their decision to live by the knowledge of good and evil separate them from God, but their human nature became hostile toward him (Genesis 1-3). Every one of us has followed in their footsteps. Paul told the Ephesians that human beings are "by nature the children of wrath" (Ephesians 2:1-3).

This means that each of us is engaged in a deep-seated, angry conflict with God. At the same time, all of us have a deep spiritual need that aches for a restored relationship with our Creator. We try to stuff that need with money, status or popularity, or we try to get other human beings to fulfill our spiritual emptiness.

The problem we face is how can finite, flawed human beings restore a relationship with the infinite Creator whom we don't see or hear with our senses? Can we climb into heaven to demand an audience with God or to negotiate peace? The obvious answer is no.

Since we can't reach God, he must reach down to us. Paul told the church in ancient Corinth:

> Now all things are of God, who has reconciled us to Himself through Jesus Christ, and has given us the ministry of reconciliation, that God was in Christ reconciling the world to Himself, not imputing their trespasses to them, and has committed to us the word of reconciliation. Now then, we are ambassadors for Christ, as though God were pleading through us; we implore you on Christ's behalf, be reconciled to God (2 Corinthians 5:18-20).

Paul doesn't claim that God simply wants to open lines of communication so we can learn to get along with him. He wants to reconcile—to heal our natural hostility toward him. He wants us to stop being his enemies and to enter into a peaceful, loving relationship with him. Only by resolving your conflict with God can you hope to heal all other broken relationships in your life at the deepest spiritual level.

Let's explore how God deals with the five basic spiritual and emotional issues that motivate destructive conflicts. Only in this way can he heal your relationship with him. We'll reverse the order from chapter one, beginning with your conflict with God.

## Solution #1: God's Answer to Our Conflict with Him

It is a false concept to believe that God accepts us just the way we are and that we can then stay just the way we are. This belief doesn't deal with the reality that we are by nature the children of wrath and the enemies of our Creator. To deal with the dysfunctional conflict in your life, you must first come to recognize your natural hostility toward God's sovereignty and your innate inability to submit to the Creator's way of life. Allowing God to heal your damaged thoughts and emotions is the only way to experience real inner peace.

A word sometimes used in the Old Testament to describe hostile human behavior is translated in English as abomination. Abomination expresses God's reaction to something that is detestable and offensive to him. A host of human behaviors and attitudes are declared abominations to God, including idolatry (Deuteronomy 7:25); homosexuality (Leviticus 18:22); witchcraft (Deuteronomy 18:10-12); and pride (Proverbs 16:5). Even a person's thoughts can be detestable to him (Proverbs 15:26). If a person refuses to heed God's instructions, then even his prayers can be an abomination to him (Proverbs 28:9).

Proverbs 6:16-19 tells us:

These six things the LORD hates, yes, seven are an abomination to Him: a proud look, a lying tongue, hands that shed innocent blood, a heart that devises wicked plans, feet that are swift in running to evil, a false witness who speaks lies, and one who sows discord among brethren.

Notice—problems of dysfunctional conflicts are listed among the human behaviors God hates. Our corrupt human nature is the source of the pride, anger, selfishness and abuse that destroys relationships. To heal your broken relationships with others, you first need to be reconciled to God and to experience a change in your hostile human nature.

In Genesis we're told that humans are made in the image of God. It records how the first human beings chose to live by the self-determined knowledge of good and evil, becoming their own gods instead of trusting their Creator. It tells us that the result of this choice is that their human nature was corrupted. All of their descendants also become corrupted. Because of our sin and alienation from God we all suffer and eventually die. What Genesis doesn't tell us is why God created us in the first place.

In Revelation, the last book of the Bible, we find the answer. The apostle John received a vision of a future time when God renews the heavens and the earth. He records God's description of the purpose for humans: "I will be his God and he shall be My son" (Revelation 21:1-7).

God created human beings in his own image because he wants children!

Humanity is a mass of wayward children who have rebelled against their Father. Kicked out of Eden, we've spent millennia destroying each other with hatred, prejudice, war and violence – all because you and I are at war with our Creator.

This seems to present us with an unsolvable problem. How can any of us, as enemies of God, negotiate peace? We can't bridge the chasm existing between us and God. Imagine yourself standing before the Grand Canyon. It is a mile deep and many miles to the other rim. God is on one side and you are on the other. What kind of running start would you need to jump the gulf between you and him?

God has to reach across the chasm to his wayward children

in order for us to be reconciled to him. This truth is central to authentic Christianity. God isn't calling people simply to accept "Jesus into their hearts" without the reality of Jesus living in their lives. His is not a gospel of "health and wealth." He is not interested in having his children participating in a set of religious rituals while refusing a change of nature. God's desire is to restore peace with his children who are in conflict with him.

Paul told the Romans, "How beautiful are the feet of those who preach the gospel of peace, and bring glad tidings of good things!" (Romans 10:15).

The gospel of peace is more than a message about the absence of violent conflict. The gospel of peace is about how God is restoring peace between him and the "children of wrath." The gospel of peace is then exhibited in how his restored children practice peacemaking among themselves.

What does it mean to be "children of wrath"? Let's look at the context in which Paul uses this phrase:

> And you He made alive, who were dead in trespasses and sins, in which you once walked according to the course of this world, according to the prince of the power of the air, the spirit who now works in the sons of disobedience, among whom also we all once conducted ourselves in the lusts of our flesh, fulfilling the desires of the flesh and of the mind, and were by nature the children of wrath, just as the others. But God, who is rich in mercy, because of His great love with which He loved us, even when we were dead in trespasses, made us alive together with Christ (by grace you have been saved) (Ephesians 2:1-5).

Because of corrupt human nature, we spend our lives trying to satisfy the selfish desires of our bodies and minds. This selfishness is counterproductive to the happiness and fulfillment we crave and actually produces suffering and conflict. God's mercy is demonstrated in his willingness to reach across the chasm that exists between him and us to reconcile his hostile children by offering them forgiveness and then giving them the ability to change their nature.

This doesn't mean that God's grace nullifies his law or justice. God's law defines sin (Romans 7:7). God gives to us the knowledge of what is right and wrong, good and evil. The law also pronounces the death penalty on those who break it (Romans 6:23). God didn't abolish his law, since that would require a change in his definition of good and evil. He also didn't declare universal, unconditional amnesty without personal repentance, since that would absolve human beings from accountability and diminish his justice.

Instead, the Father chose to send his Son to live as a perfect human being, and to die as the substitute for us, thereby paying our required penalty (John 1:1-18). God's justice pronounced the death penalty on rebellious humanity. His love satisfied his justice through the surrogate sacrifice of Jesus, who was then resurrected to return to the throne of God, where he would act as intercessor between God and humankind. It is in the life, death, resurrection and work of Christ that God is resolving the conflict between him and corrupt humanity.

> Inasmuch then as the children have partaken of flesh and blood, He Himself likewise shared in the same, that through death He might destroy him who had the power of death, that is, the devil, and release those who through fear of death were all their lifetime subject to bondage. For indeed He does not give aid to angels, but He does give aid to the seed of Abraham. Therefore, in all things He had to be made like His brethren, that He might be a merciful and faithful High Priest in things pertaining to God to make propitiation for the sins of the people. For

in that He Himself has suffered, being tempted, He is able to aid those who are tempted (Hebrews 2:14-18).

God reaches across the chasm to his enemies, offering them forgiveness and relationship. In God's plan to bridge this enormous gap, Jesus Christ "had to be made like his brethren." To understand how the "children of wrath" are reconciled to God, we must try to wrap our minds around the reality of Christ divesting himself of the privileges of divinity and becoming human (Philippians 2:5-11). By taking this conscious action, he experienced what it is like to feel tired, to suffer hunger and to endure physical pain. His muscles ached from swinging a carpenter's hammer, and his body got sweaty and dirty from walking the dusty roads of Judea. He suffered the emotional hurt of being publically mocked, abandoned by friends, unjustly accused and brutally murdered. He endured all this in order to reconcile to God those who are his enemies.

For it pleased the Father that in Him all the fullness should dwell, and by Him to reconcile all things to Himself, by Him, whether things on earth or things in heaven, having made peace through the blood of His cross. And you, who once were alienated and enemies in your mind by wicked works, yet now He has reconciled in the body of His flesh through death, to present you holy, and blameless, and above reproach in His sight (Colossians 1:19-22).

Paul wrote to the Christians in Rome:

For when we were still without strength, in due time Christ died for the ungodly. For scarcely for a righteous man will one die; yet perhaps for a good man someone would even dare to die. But God demonstrates His own love toward us, in that while we were yet sinners, Christ died for us. Much more then, having now been justified by His blood, we shall be saved from wrath through Him. For if when we were enemies we were reconciled to God through the death of His Son, much more, having been reconciled, we shall be saved by His life (Romans 5:6-10).

God reached out to reconcile his wayward children before we knew him or repented of our sins. Christ submitted to being a substitute sacrifice for us while we were still enemies. In these actions we get a glimpse of God's awe-inspiring love toward us even though we are acting as abominations toward him.

Let's put Paul's words about someone dying for a righteous man in a modern context. There are numerous accounts of a soldier in combat jumping on a grenade to save his buddies. In a modern analogy, Jesus jumped on the grenade to save those who hated him, tortured him and deserved his distain.

One of the most detailed Old Testament Messianic prophecies is recorded in Isaiah 52:13-53:12. The prophecy describes the Servant of God as physically indiscernible from other men. His life is filled with sorrow and grief. He is rejected, scorned and killed for the sins of humanity. The prophecy contains this remarkable insight: "Yet it pleased the LORD to bruise Him; He has put Him to grief"

When the Son of God crossed the chasm between God and humankind, he supplied the way for healing the core issues that cause dysfunctional conflict. This was pleasing to God.

Only by responding to God's love and forgiveness can we have any hope of escaping the eternal penalty of sin, being restored into a peaceful relationship with God and having the ability to deal with the spiritual aspects of conflict.

## Solution #2: God's Answer to Pride

Pride, the exaggerated view of self, keeps us from both accepting responsibility for hurting others and forgiving others when they hurt us. We want payback. We want to win. We want others to recognize our goodness. We want to defend our "honor." Jesus taught a different attitude: "Blessed are the poor in spirit, for theirs is the kingdom of heaven."

Being poor in spirit doesn't mean walking around feeling depressed. To be poor in spirit is to know your spiritual and emotional poverty without God in your life. When you are poor in spirit, you see the Creator's greatness and you are acutely aware of your absolute dependency on him.

Jesus told a parable about a Pharisee, a member of a respected religious group, and a tax collector. Jewish society ostracized tax collectors because they assisted the occupying Roman government. The two men in the parable went to the Jewish temple to pray.

The Pharisee thanked God for his spiritual superiority. He reminded God that he wasn't dishonest or unjust, nor was he an adulterer or a collaborator like the tax collector. He took great satisfaction in himself as a man who worshipped God and paid his tithes. The tax collector, in realization of his unworthiness before God, "beat his breast saying, 'God be merciful to me a sinner!'" (Luke 18:9-14).

Luke said that Jesus spoke this parable because of those people who trusted in themselves that they were righteous while despising others. He taught that God accepted the prayer of the tax collector and rejected the prayer of the Pharisee. Jesus didn't say that God accepts dishonesty or adultery, nor did he say that we shouldn't pay tithes. The purpose of the parable is to pinpoint two great areas of religious pride: measuring our righteousness by the actions of other people, and despising others by feeling superior to them.

The Pharisee took great pride in his own definition of spiritual enlightenment; the tax collector recognized his spiritual poverty without God. In the end, it was the tax collector who was blessed by God.

It is not easy to recognize our spiritual poverty. Each of us is like a little child yelling "Me do it! Me do it!" at the adult who is trying to help until the child finally collapses in tearful frustration. Only when we accept our spiritual failure, our innate hostility toward God, and our need for his love and guidance can we finally say to him, "Father, please forgive me and teach me how to live."

You can try to ignore God. You can work hard, play hard and pretend you're indestructible. You can act "religious" without really relating to God in your everyday life, but eventually you will have to come face-to-face with how short, and ultimately how meaningless, your life is without him.

Theodore Roosevelt has always been a fascinating person to me. A close friend of Roosevelt, William Beebe, wrote that after a long day of discussion, he and Teddy went outside to study the majesty of the stars and galaxies in the night sky. After a long silence Roosevelt said, 'Now, I think we are small enough. Let's go to bed.'" In our fast-paced lifestyles we don't take the time to witness God's majesty in his creation. The brilliance of God, revealed in his creation, causes us to appreciate our smallness before his greatness and goodness.

When you experience the utter poverty of life without God, fully appreciate his way of reconciling with you as his enemy, and recognize your own inability to cross the chasm between you and God, then you can have the humility to see others as weak, spiritually impoverished, wayward children of God in need of being reconciled to their Creator. Only then can you recognize God's power of forgiveness as a way to help another person to repent. Then you can begin to offer forgiveness as a way to help someone who has sinned against you or ask forgiveness from someone else.

## Solution #3:
## God's Answer to Our Need for Control

We have a natural desire to protect our rights, self-image and emotional security. We resist God's instructions because we will do almost anything to maintain independent control over our own lives so we can avoid discomfort. We actually see ourselves as independent gods and goddesses dispensing our own versions of justice and of how people should relate to us. Our response to God's offer of reconciliation must include giving up worshipping at the feet of a self-made image and submitting to the re-creation of our nature. Only then can we fulfill our original purpose as his children.

You must come to understand the uselessness of trying to control everything in your life and you must accept your complete dependency on God. This doesn't mean that you give up personal responsibility for making decisions. It means that you accept a radically different set of standards for decision making and conflict resolution. It means giving up your hostility toward God and accepting your spiritual poverty. It means hungering for his interaction in your life.

A Canaanite woman came to Jesus asking for her daughter to be healed. Imagine her surprise when Jesus ignored her. His disciples asked Jesus to send her away. Jesus finally addressed her by saying, "It is not good to take the children's bread and give it to the little dogs." If anyone ever had the right to feel offended, this woman surely did. Jesus, the one many claimed was the Messiah, was ignoring her. His disciples were rude and seemed prejudiced against Canaanites. She could have become disillusioned, claiming Jesus to be a fraud.

Instead, she answered, "True, Lord, yet even the little dogs eat the crumbs which fall from their masters' table." Jesus commended her faith and healed her daughter (Matthew 15:21-28). The

Canaanite woman's faith couldn't be swayed by the actions of others. She was too aware of her total dependency upon God. By understanding her own spiritual poverty she remained unaffected by the actions and perceived putdowns of others. She trusted that God would work out what was best for her and her daughter.

Faith is more than belief in the existence of God or an acceptance of forgiveness. Faith is trust in God's goodness and love. It is trust in God's instructions leading to a loving response of obedience, even when those instructions don't make sense to the natural mind. Ultimately, faith is turning control of your life over to God.

## Solution #4:
## God's Answer to Our Need to Satisfy Our Desires

In his epistle, James asks:

> Where do wars and fights come from among you? Do they not come from your desires for pleasure that war in your members? You lust and you do not have. You murder and covet and do not obtain. You fight and war. Yet you do not have because you do not ask. You ask and you do not receive because you ask amiss, that you may spend it on your pleasures. Adulterers and adulteresses! Do you not know that friendship with the world is enmity with God? Whoever wants to make himself the friend of the world makes himself the enemy of God (James 4:1-5).

Here James explains why there is so much conflict between people, and between us and God. Many times it is because we are obsessed with getting others to fulfill our every desire. God is seen as a genie in a bottle whose main purpose is to make us happy by meeting our demands. Unless we accept God's standards and give up this selfishness, we will continue to see him as an enemy who is somehow keeping us from happiness. Think about it. Do you feel that obeying God will keep you from experiencing fun and happiness? We are designed to experience an obedient relationship with God. At the same time we want to maintain god-like control over our own decisions about right and wrong. We want to protect our rights, self-image and emotional security by forcing others to meet our demands. We want to satisfy the "lust of the flesh, the lust of the eyes and the pride of life" without any personal accountability, and we do not want to suffer any negative consequences for our actions. With all these conflicting motives, no wonder we're such a mess.

James writes that these incompatible desires create "fights and wars." He goes on to state that many times we don't receive God's blessings because we don't ask him, and when we do ask he doesn't grant our requests because our requests are selfish. In the final analysis, the apostle returns to the core problem—we fight among ourselves because we are in conflict with God.

God's answers to the conflicts caused by our own desires are found in the Sermon on the Mount. Jesus begins by explaining attitudes that are essential to becoming a child of God (Matthew 5:3-10). He says that those who are the children of God:

- are poor in spirit instead of self-righteous
- mourn instead of acting with selfish abandonment and no concern for sin
- are meek instead of arrogant
- hunger and thirst after righteousness instead of being spiritually complacent
- are merciful instead of being vengeful
- are pure in heart instead of being hypocritical

- are peacemakers instead of conflict makers
- are willing to be persecuted for doing what is right before God.

We can't solve our conflicts with others until we resolve the conflicts within our own minds. In the Beatitudes, Jesus summarizes both the causes and remedies for human conflict with God and each other. Studying this list is the starting point for self-examination in any conflict we have with others.

A person once told me that a counselor claimed that internal conflicts stemmed from resisting natural desires and trying to obey the Bible. This secular counselor advised his client to give in to desires and to give up attempts to obey biblical instructions. The counselor claimed the internal struggles would disappear. This is natural thinking for a person in conflict with his Creator.

How can you have the power to work through your conflicted desires? The answer lies in how God heals our damaged human nature. This requires his personal involvement and our response known as repentance.

## Repentance

The biblical concept of repentance is a reasoned understanding and acceptance of God's standards of good and evil, coupled with feelings of regret for living in rebellion against those standards. It is recognizing that you are a marred image of the Creator and desperately in need of being restored into a relationship with him.

This understanding will motivate you to turn away from self-determination and actions contrary to God. These contrary thoughts and actions are called sin. In turning away from self-determination, you can turn to God and begin a new life. Repentance is more than the intellectual acceptance of Jesus

Christ, and it is more than conversion to a set of beliefs. It is a total commitment to becoming a restored child of God and a disciple of Jesus.

Just because God, through Christ, reached across the chasm to offer reconciliation doesn't mean that we are suddenly no longer "by nature the children of wrath." Repentance involves accepting the need to have your nature changed. It leads to obedience to God's instructions about how life is supposed to work.

God wants more in your life than just behavior modification. He wants to change your corrupt nature. But how can human beings experience a change in nature?

The apostle Paul looked at the unique qualities of human beings and realized that there is a "spirit in man" that makes us dramatically different from animals. This is another way of expressing that human beings are made in the image of God. It is this unique aspect of human beings that gives us the ability to do geometry, to write a song or to experience empathy.

He explained to the Corinthians:

> For what man knows the things of a man except the spirit of man that is in him? Even so no one knows the things of God except the Spirit of God. Now we have received, not the spirit of the world, but the Spirit who is from God, that we might know the things that have been freely given to us by God (1 Corinthians 2:11-12).

Paul did not encourage his readers to explore the secrets of finding the god within. Human beings may be made in the "image of God," but we are incomplete creations. The apostle, who wrote to the Romans that the natural mind is the enemy of God, taught the Corinthians that the human mind by itself is inadequate to know the spiritual ways of God: "But the natural man does not receive the things of the Spirit of God, for they are foolishness to him; nor can he know them, because they are spiritually discerned" (I Corinthians 2:13-16).

Christ crossed the chasm to offer reconciliation. The required human response to God's grace is repentance. God must then introduce his Spirit into a union with the human spirit in order to launch the transformation from being "children of wrath" to becoming children of God. Jesus is the divine nature exhibited in uncorrupted human nature. God, through his Spirit, now introduces the divine nature into corrupt human nature in us (2 Peter 1:2-4).

To be authentic, Christianity must involve a change in nature. Through God's Spirit, you can begin to have your old nature changed into the new nature of a child of God. Paul wrote to the Romans:

> For you did not receive the spirit of bondage again to fear, but you received the Spirit of adoption by whom we cry out, 'Abba, Father.' The Spirit Himself bears witness with our spirit that we are the children of God, and if children, then heirs—heirs of God and joint heirs with Christ, if indeed we suffer with Him, that we may be glorified together (Romans 8:15-17).

The dilemma of introducing God's divine nature into corrupt human nature is that we will experience intense internal struggles as our own nature resists his nature. Religious tracts, claiming that a simple prayer and acceptance of Jesus produces eternal salvation, and that nothing else is needed, reduce Christ's sacrifice to cheap grace and the Christian life to a label without substance.

The first step of salvation is accepting Christ's sacrifice as a substitute for the eternal death we deserve. God's work of salvation in us involves much more than our simple acceptance of this sacrifice. Salvation is the way God is saving us from death and recreating us according to our original purpose—to be his children.

Authentic Christianity involves the struggle to submit to God's nature. This struggle will continue all the days of our physical lives. Spirit filled Christians will have moments of faith and moments of doubt; times when we will resist temptation and times when we will succumb to sin; times when we will handle conflict in a Christ-like way and times when we will offend or struggle with forgiveness. The end result of this struggle is that God will change our nature.

## Solution #5:
## God's Answer to Our Need for Emotional Healing

Typical human forgiveness is passive. As the injured party, we wait for the offender to admit wrong and to tell us, "I'm sorry." We think that only then can we experience emotional healing, and only then can we offer forgiveness.

God's forgiveness is active. Christ died for us while we were yet sinners. As the injured party, God isn't passively waiting for us to repent so he can be healed and then offer forgiveness. Because God has no need to be healed, he is actively seeking to reconcile with us, offering us forgiveness and helping us repent so that **we** can be healed.

Human forgiveness is based on the injured party needing to be healed through the repentance of the offender. Since God is absolute love, a being without need of emotional healing, he offers reconciliation solely through love for the offender. This doesn't mean that the offender is excused from the responsibility to repent. Reconciliation is a two-way street, but it is God who initiates the reconciliation process.

Because God is actively offering his forgiveness, and Jesus Christ suffered for our restoration, we are drawn by God's goodness to repent and to be reconciled. Paul writes, "Or do you despise the riches of His goodness, forbearance, and longsuffering, not knowing that the goodness of God leads you to repentance?" (Romans 2:4).

When we experience spiritual, mental and emotional healing through God's mercy and forgiveness, we receive the power to change the way we treat those who have offended us. We are free to be open to reconciliation, even with an offender who is not ready to say, "I'm sorry." Our desire will be to lead the other person to healing and reconciliation with God. This is the first step of the *mercy effect.*

# 3

# The Healing Process:
# Message to the Injured Person

Why begin with a message to the injured person? You may be thinking, "Shouldn't you begin with a stern correction of the one who did the wrong? Isn't the starting point of reconciliation an apology from the offender? If the offender doesn't apologize, how can we force him or her to the negotiating table? What about justice?"

These questions beg an answer. However, if this is your starting point as an offended person, you will have a difficult time achieving meaningful reconciliation because of the intensity of your emotions.

We begin with instructions for the offended person because many Christians have sadly walked away from lifelong friendships, divorced mates, watched their congregations disintegrate because of political in-fighting, or even given up on God because of offenses committed by fellow Christians. Being offended by the wrong conduct of another Christian is one of the greatest destroyers of faith and commitment to the teachings of Jesus.

Since God is creating a family, the first goal in resolving any conflict among Christians should be restoring our relationships as spiritual brothers and sisters. The issues, which are worked out through wisdom, open communication and principles of conflict management, can be solved only if the goal is to create restored relationships as children of God. Reconciliation involves forgiveness on the part of the offended person and repentance on the part of the offender. Only then can individuals deal with the issues of disagreement.

Repentance is the required human response for an offender who has sinned against God or a brother. For a relationship to be restored completely, the offender must take responsibility for his or her wrongdoing.

Forgiveness is the required Christ-like response of the injured person toward the offender. One of the most destructive forces in a Christian's spiritual life can be the emotional pain caused by the sin of another Christian. The anguish and frustration can lead an offended person to obsession, depression and bitterness.

Let's explore the five causes of dysfunctional conflict in light of God's instructions to his children when they have been marginalized, insulted or abused; and then let's look at how we should deal with the offenders in each case.

## Solution #1:
## First Seek to be Reconciled to God

When someone has sinned against you, what is the first step toward reconciliation? Should you confront the person and explain the offense? Should you ask God to enforce justice and to punish the offender? Should you forgive the person and go on as though nothing happened?

To answer these questions, we must first deal with the concept of forgiveness. We've already seen that God offers forgiveness to his wayward children while we are still his enemies. We've also seen that for a relationship to be established, God requires us to repent of our rebelliousness, sins and hostility toward him. Reconciliation is a two-way street.

Forgiveness doesn't mean ignoring the offense or erasing God's standards of right and wrong. Rather, forgiveness means giving up the preoccupation to make the other person meet our expectations or suffer punishment. It involves deciding not to obsess over the offense or to gossip about it to others, and it means letting go of the animosity and distress that can lead to emotional dysfunction. Among disciples of Jesus Christ, forgiveness begins with desiring to restore our relationships as spiritual brothers and sisters, and being willing to work towards reconciliation.

When you are sick or injured, all you can think about is relieving your pain and suffering. It is natural for a person who is sick for a long time to become emotionally consumed by his or her illness. It is the same way with emotional hurt. The emotions feel like an open wound. We want the other person to make things right or to be punished for hurting us. When neither happens to the level of our expectations, then we can obsess about our emotional pain.

Forgiveness doesn't mean you excuse the other person's actions or deny your emotional distress. It does mean that you give up your demands for satisfaction, preoccupation with the hurt and drive for revenge. It also means being willing to reach across the gap that has been created between you and the offender.

Peter, one of Jesus' disciples, wanted to know how many times he should forgive someone who had mistreated him. Peter asked if seven times was sufficient. What a remarkable attitude! It's hard enough to forgive someone who has mistreated you one time. Forgiving that person two or three times would require you to be a spiritual giant. Peter asked if seven times was sufficient. Jesus said to forgive *seventy times seven*.

Jesus illustrates his point with a parable about a man who owed a king an enormous sum of money. The king demanded payment. The man was bankrupt and could not pay his debt. He begged for forgiveness and the king showed him mercy by erasing the account.

The forgiven man left the king and came upon someone who owed him a small amount of money, but couldn't pay. Instead of forgiving the small debt, the forgiven man had the poor man thrown into prison. The king heard about the situation and called the man he forgave into his presence. The king told the forgiven man how he should have had "compassion on your fellow servant, just as I had compassion on you." In Jesus' parable, because the forgiven man had been shown mercy, but then refused to show mercy to others, he is punished.

Jesus then makes this extraordinary statement: "So my Heavenly Father also will do to you if each of you, from his heart, does not forgive his brother his trespasses." To accept God's forgiveness while refusing to forgive others results in God withdrawing his mercy from you (Matthew 18:21-35). This can be a hard road for the offended person who struggles with emotional pain and expects closure with the offender.

When you obsess over an offense, you become driven by hurt, anger and bitterness. When you allow anger and bitterness to control your life, you erect a barrier between you and God. This means that the first step in dealing with someone who has sinned against you is to recognize **your** poverty before God. This is difficult and can take much prayer time both in asking God for healing and in dealing with the offender.

Two things happen when you refuse to open your heart to forgive someone who has sinned against you. First, as I just mentioned, you erect a barrier between you and God. The strength to forgive others springs from remembering how God sent Christ across the chasm to forgive you while you were still an enemy.

Paul tells the Colossians:

Therefore, as the elect of God, holy and beloved, put on tender mercies, kindness, humility, meekness, longsuffering; bearing with one another, and forgiving one another, if anyone has a complaint against another; even as Christ forgave you, so you also must do. But above all these things put on love, which is the bond of perfection. And let the peace of God rule in your hearts (Colossians 3:12-15).

Second, refusing to forgive traps you in the emotional moment of the offense. You relive the incident over and over again like watching a rerun of an old movie. The offense becomes ingrained into your thought processes until you are consumed with a need for the offender to heal you by apologizing or by suffering punishment. The more you obsess over an offense, the more difficult it is for you to show love in other areas of your life. I've seen people whose preoccupation with an offense led them to conclude that there are only two kinds of people in the world—those who agree with them by sharing their bitterness— or wrongheaded (even evil) people who either side with the offender or try to remain neutral.

You begin to lay the foundation for real spiritual peace only after you accept and trust in God's good will to work out what is best for your life, in spite of difficulties and offenses. When you are at peace with God, you find that you are not easily offended. Instead, you will quickly overlook minor offenses because of an acute awareness of how God forgives you.

"The discretion of a man makes him slow to anger, and his glory is to overlook a transgression" (Proverbs 19:11). Solomon's instructions can help you avoid a lot of sleepless nights fixating on how someone didn't treat you the way you wanted to be treated.

## The Way of Peace

This doesn't mean that spiritual peace is infused into us like an intravenous miracle drug. When someone mistreats you the resulting frustration, anger and feeling of betrayal can be difficult to manage. It also takes time to heal from the hurt.

When we trust in God, we can learn the way of peace, and then choose to live that way. God, through the prophet Isaiah, warns the people of ancient Israel: "The way of peace they have not known, and there is no justice in their ways; they have made themselves crooked paths; whoever takes that way shall not know peace" (see Isaiah 59:1-8).

How can we learn the way of peace? The way of peace requires that we change the way we think. Each of us is the sum of our thoughts. It is easy to become mental slaves to the demands of the moment, to negative emotions and to the information overload of mass media. It is also easy to succumb to the attractiveness of a self-absorbed, consumer society.

Here's a simple method to experience more peace in your busy, stress-filled life. Take time throughout the day to shut off the computer, cell-phone, radio and television; physically relax in a place where you have no distractions; and spend time finding peace in prayer and Bible study. Remember, the "way of peace" begins with reconciliation to your Creator, followed by filling your mind with his ways and his thoughts.

It is important to remember that emotions are changed by first changing thoughts. What do you choose to think about before you go to sleep at night and when you first wake up in the morning? Do you see everything in life as negative and bad? Do you obsess on how people have mistreated you and will mistreat you in the future? Instead, try beginning each day by clearing your mind of all worries and anxieties, and think about God's blessings and his ways.

Paul instructed the church at Philippi:

> Be anxious for nothing, but in everything by prayer and supplication, with thanksgiving, let your requests be known to God; and the peace of God, which surpasses all understanding, will guard your hearts and minds

through Christ Jesus. Finally, brethren, whatever things are true, whatever things are noble, whatever things are just, whatever things are pure, whatever things are lovely, whatever things are of good report, if there is any virtue and if there is anything praiseworthy—meditate on these things (Philippians 4:6-8).

In my life I have at times found excuses for not thinking on the things that are true, noble, just, pure and lovely. Have you ever considered how embarrassing it would be if your thoughts were spelled out across your forehead like a scrolling digital sign for all to read? If this happened, we'd all be more guarded in what we are thinking. Others may not know our thoughts, but God does, and it is our thoughts that ultimately determine our attitudes, our emotional responses and our actions.

Accepting the freedom and power of God's mercy gives you the strength to forgive others. When you accept God's forgiveness, the emphasis of your relationships shifts from how others treat you to how you treat others. The way you think about others will also change. This is the mercy effect in action.

## Solution #2:
### Seek Humility: It's not Always about Winning

Isaac was the leader of a nomadic tribe with large herds of animals. The Philistines had filled in wells previously dug by his father Abraham. Isaac re-dug the wells for his family and flocks. He also discovered another source of running water. Some of the nomadic herdsmen argued with Isaac's herdsmen about this new source of life-giving water.

Isaac could have claimed he had a right to this well because God had given the land to his family; or that he had a right to it because his servants had done the work; or that the other herdsmen could purchase water from him. Instead, he avoided conflict by moving on and digging another well, only to be confronted by the herdsmen in that area.

Once again, Isaac decided not to call his men to arms, inciting possible resentment or even violence. Water is vital for life and he understood the needs of the other people in the area. He also realized that he would have to live with these people, and that a feud could last for generations. He dug yet another well. This time no one questioned his claim. Isaac lived in peace with his neighbors declaring, "For now the LORD has made room for us, and we shall be fruitful in the land" (Genesis 26:17-22).

When struggling with the need to win over the other person it is a good time to return to the Beatitudes. What does it really mean to be pure in spirit, to mourn spiritually, to be meek, to hunger and thirst after righteousness, to be merciful, to be pure in heart and to be peacemakers? The only way to understand these profound spiritual principles is to ask God to give you both the understanding and the power to experience these attitudes.

There are times in life when God expects us to make personal stands on moral principles. Being a peacemaker doesn't mean compromising with right and wrong. When we obey God we will at times find ourselves in conflict with much of society. These kinds of conflicts aren't about "winning" but about having the integrity to live by Christian principles.

God also doesn't expect us to be doormats for bullies. We are to "turn the other cheek," but this doesn't mean allowing people to abuse us verbally or physically, and to do so repeatedly. There are situations in which people must be confronted or avoided.

But how many needless conflicts could be avoided just by remembering—it's not always about winning. Personal scorecards don't matter in the eyes of God.

### Solution #3: Give Up Your Need to Control the Response of the Other Person

When you have been offended, giving up your need to control the response of the offender is a difficult process. The fear is that if you give up control, then the other person will get away with his or her wrongdoing.

When you have an emotional need to control the response of the offender, and it appears that justice is delayed, you may find yourself easily motivated by vengeance. It is important to understand the difference between justice and vengeance. Justice is concerned with doing what is right and lawful. There are moral consequences for wrong actions.

Vengeance is concerned with your need to control the response of the offender and to get payback. Vengeance motivates you to take actions that cause emotional harm to the person who has hurt you. These actions usually escalate and can cause damage to innocent bystanders. How many times have we seen the bitter conflict between parents create deep insecurities, anger and behavioral problems in their children? Parents, in fulfilling their need to hurt each other, place their innocent children in harm's way. Children become the "collateral damage" of their parent's personal war.

Paul wrote to the church in Rome about vengeance:

Repay no one evil for evil. Have regard for good things in the sight of all men. If it is possible, as much as it depends upon you, live peaceably with all men. Beloved, do not avenge yourselves, but rather give place to wrath; for it is written, 'Vengeance is Mine, I will repay,' says the Lord. Therefore, 'If your enemy is hungry, feed him; If he is thirsty, give him a drink; for in doing so you will heap coals of fire upon his head.' Do not be overcome by evil, but overcome evil with good (Romans 12:17-21).

It is not always possible to live peaceably with another person. Some people are going to repay good with evil. In our narcissistic society, some people will always act selfishly. Paul instructs Christians to do their part in being peaceful, not allowing themselves to be overcome by another's sin by responding with sin. (We'll take a look at irreconcilable conflict with an antagonist in a later chapter). The biblical story of Absalom is an example of how the need for vengeance can lead to disastrous results. Ancient Israel's King David had a harem (a common practice for ancient kings in the Middle East) that produced a large number of children. Imagine the conflicts breaking out among wives and siblings all competing for David's attention.

One of David's sons, named Amnon, fell in love with his half-sister Tamar. Tamar resisted her half-brother's advances until he finally overcame her and forced her to have sex with him. When the news reached the king he was angry, yet he acted indecisively. Two years passed and still David did nothing. Maybe he was trying to avoid a public scandal. Maybe he felt guilty about not being a good father. Maybe he couldn't get past his own hurt over the incident, but the end result is he did nothing.

Absalom, another of David's sons, tired of waiting for his father to take action, avenged his sister by killing Amnon. In many ways, it would seem that Absalom is the hero of the story. He avenges his sister and supports her for the rest of his life, while David seems unconcerned or incompetent. Envision Absalom's deep disappointment when, instead of being hailed as a hero, his father exiled him from the country for three lonely, desperate years.

David eventually extended amnesty to his son, but for Absalom, the seeds of discontent, the feeling that he had been wronged, the belief that he was a victim of David's ineptitude, had burrowed deep into the core of his being. Motivated by a need to share his discontent, he began to feed his frustration to others. Absalom ultimately launched a coup to overthrow King David and was killed by the commander of David's army.

Absalom's self-destruction was tragic. His actions, however, were predictable. His sister had been wronged, but justice was delayed. Motivated by vengeance, he took matters into his own hands, only to face banishment by his father. Soon he became convinced that he had been wronged by David. He couldn't forgive his father's incompetence. Absalom began to see himself as a victim. His anger against David became all-consuming, so he tried to overthrow his father's kingdom only to suffer defeat and death.

The story of Absalom warns us of three major lessons we need to remember when we have been offended.

- The first lesson is to be very careful about picking your time, place and method of confronting an offender. No matter how right Absolom's cause may have appeared, he couldn't win his case by overthrowing the king who had been appointed by God and represented the very law by which he was seeking justice. He needed to work within the law.

- The second point is that you can't stew on an offense until it consumes your thoughts and emotions.

- The third lesson is that there are times when an offender will not repent. In this case Absalom needed to take his case to God. Absalom didn't trust in God's justice and timing, but instead demanded action on his own timetable. The result was that he ended up committing actions as wrong as Amnon's crimes.

There are times when confrontation will only spread the conflict and damage the innocent. In these cases, you must consider whether the right action is to endure the wrong for the good of others by applying Peter's admonishment:

For this is commendable, if because of conscience toward God one endures grief, suffering wrongfully. For what credit is it if, when you are beaten for your faults, you take it patiently? But when you do good and suffer, if you take it patiently, this is commendable before God. For to this you were called, because Christ also suffered for us, leaving us an example, that you should follow His steps: 'Who committed no sin, Nor was deceit found in His mouth;' who, when He was reviled, did not revile in return; when He suffered, He did not threaten, but committed Himself to Him who judges righteously (1 Peter 2:19-23).

In these instances, we find ourselves returning to the need to be at peace with God and trusting in his justice, mercy and wisdom. It is by crying out to him for inner peace, and committing our life to obeying his ways, that we find the strength to deal with the offenses committed against us.

### Solution #4: Seek God's Solution Instead of Fulfilling Your Desires and Expectations

Pause before you react to the offender. You need to ask yourself, "Why am I offended?" In answering this question, you will be faced with one of the most difficult aspects of corrupted human nature—lack of intellectual honesty.

We like to think that we are objective, but all of us filter situations through our own emotions, personalities and desires. All of us live under the illusion that our subjectivity is objective. That's why you must turn to God's Word as the objective standard. When offended, you need to find a quiet place so you can honestly ask yourself some difficult questions. You may find it helpful to write down the following questions and your answers:

- What is the Christ-like response to the situation? (Before you impose your solution on a situation involving someone who has sinned against you, seek God's solution.)

- What lessons can God teach through this situation?

- Am I overreacting to a misunderstanding?

- Am I reacting out of frustration because I am requiring the other person to fulfill my expectations?

- Am I angry because my pride is injured?

- Is this an offense that I should simply overlook? Maybe the person is under great stress and her outburst of anger is not typical behavior, so I should choose to forgive and to forget.

- How did I contribute to this conflict? I can imagine some readers thinking, "What? Analyze my contribution to the problem? I'm the one who was wronged."

(For a more complete self-evaluation, see *The Peacemaker* by Ken Sande, Baker Books, 2004.)

It is important to answer these questions prayerfully before going to the offender. The last question is one we often overlook. You must analyze even the smallest ways you may have contributed to the problem, and then be willing to acknowledge and amend your part.

Jesus gives these instructions on what to do before approaching a sinning brother:

And why do you look at the speck in your brother's eye, but do not consider the plank in your own eye? Or how can you say to your brother, 'Let me remove the speck from your eye'; and look, a plank is in your own eye? Hypocrite! First remove the plank from your own eye, and then you will see clearly to remove the speck from your brother's eye (Matthew 7:3-5).

The hyperbole is obvious. A person is trying to remove a grain of sawdust from a brother's eye while causing mayhem because a two-by-four is sticking out of his eye. Jesus doesn't teach us to ignore our brother's sin. His point is that before we approach a brother, we must first be reconciled to God, repenting of our own sins.

We must then adopt the right attitude as we explore how we may have contributed to the problem.

## Solution #5:
## Seek God's Healing of Your Damaged Emotions

Once we ask God to heal our damaged emotions, then we must seek to follow Christ's example in reaching out to the offender. We return to the core concept that Christ died for us while we were still his enemies. To follow his example means to offer forgiveness in a spirit of reconciliation. In Luke 6:27-36 we find some of Jesus' most difficult teachings concerning our reactions to those who misuse us:

> But I say to you who hear: Love your enemies, do good to those who hate you, bless those who curse you, and pray for those who spitefully use you (Luke 6:27-28).

> But if you love those who love you, what credit is that to you? For even sinners love those who love them. And if you do good to those who do good to you, what credit is that to you? For even sinners do the same (Luke 6:32-33).

> But love your enemies, do good, and lend, hoping for nothing in return; and your reward will be great, and you will be the sons of the Most High. For He is kind to the unthankful and evil. Therefore be merciful, just as your Father also is merciful (Luke 6:35-36).

Jesus is teaching his disciples the same proactive approach to offenders he exhibited in reconciling hostile, wayward children to God. By following his example, we exhibit the gospel to others.

Think of the wayward son in Jesus' parable of The Prodigal Son. He returned home only after his life had deteriorated to the point that he was eating swill with the hogs. Sharing the gospel is one wayward child who wasted his life eating with the hogs, telling another wayward hog-swill-eating child how to get out of the trough so he too can return home.

When you obsess on the offense, trapping yourself in the pain of the moment, you'll find it is impossible to reach out to the offender. This is why you must ask God to heal your emotions, and to change the way you think about the situation. Conflict that has caused deep wounds takes time and effort to heal. Sometimes you must step back from the situation, giving yourself time to think through the problem, and time to get control of your anger, disappointment, frustration and feelings of betrayal. You must take time to experience a profound reconciliation with God before you deal with the offender.

Before we discuss the offending person, there are a number of emotional traps we must avoid in order to experience emotional healing. These emotional traps can have dire spiritual consequences.

# 4

# Spiritual and Emotional Traps

The most difficult part of working through conflict is the emotions we experience. We must work though the danger of becoming trapped in a dysfunctional emotional state of hurt, anger and bitterness. This emotional trap can affect our other relationships and create a barrier between us and God.

Here are a number of spiritual and emotional traps to work through in dealing with conflict.

## Allowing Yourself to Be Controlled by Anger

All anger is not destructive. God experiences anger (Psalm 7:11). Paul wrote in Ephesians 4:26, "Be you angry, and do not sin." However, we must be careful not to confuse rational anger with typical dysfunctional human anger.

Solomon wrote, "An angry man stirs up strife, and a furious man abounds in transgressions" (Proverbs 29:22).

How each of us experiences and handles anger is rooted in our biological makeup and life experiences. Paul's description of corrupt humans as "the children of wrath" is insightful. This phrase highlights our natural hostility, which leads to destructive anger and violent confrontations. Here are seven points to think about when dealing with anger:

- "'Be angry, and do not sin': do not let the sun go down on your wrath" (Ephesians 4:26). Righteous anger is short-lived and doesn't lead to vengeful, retaliatory actions.

- "...nor give place to the devil" (Ephesians 4:27). A person experiencing righteous anger controls his or her own emotions and isn't manipulated by Satan.

- Righteous anger is experienced when there is a moral principle involved. Unfortunately, most of our anger is generated when we feel that our rights have been violated, self-image threatened or emotional security damaged. Or we may simply be angry because of hurt pride.

- A person who has righteous anger gets angry at situations. He's not angry all the time. On the other hand, a person expecting a fight is generally going to find one. The book of Proverbs contains numerous insights into anger:

  o "The desire of the righteous is only good, but the expectation of the wicked is wrath" (Proverbs 11:23).

  o "He who is slow to wrath has great understanding, but he who is impulsive exalts folly" (Proverbs 14:29).

  o "He who is slow to anger is better than the mighty, and he who rules his spirit than he who takes a city" (Proverbs 16:32).

  o "A man of great wrath will suffer punishment; for if you rescue him, you will have to do it again" (Proverbs 19:19).

  o "Make no friendship with an angry man, and with a furious man do not go, lest you learn his ways and set a snare for your soul" (Proverbs 22:24-25).

- Righteous anger is used to energize positive actions. Jesus went to a synagogue where he found a man with a withered hand. Some of the Pharisees watched to see whether Jesus would heal the crippled man so they could accuse him of working on the Sabbath. Jesus asked them, "Is it lawful on the Sabbath to do good or to do evil, to save life or kill?" The Pharisees knew his argument was sound, so they kept silent.

Jesus was angry at their self-righteousness and lack of compassion. How would you have handled the situation? My first inclination would have been to tell the Pharisees to stretch out their hands and I would have withered their hands left and right. I would have taught them a lesson or two about loving their neighbor.

This wasn't the reaction of Jesus. He asked the crippled man to stretch out his hand, and Jesus healed it. Jesus' anger motivated him to take positive action. The anger of the Pharisees motivated them to plot to kill Jesus (Mark 3:1-6).

- Righteous anger doesn't generate hatred. Hatred is a strong desire for the destruction of the other person's well-being without any offer of forgiveness, reconciliation and peace. Jesus was angry with the Pharisees, and at times he declared that they were in danger of suffering God's justice, but he was always open to their repentance and reconciliation.

- Righteous anger doesn't produce depression or self-destructive actions. Self-cutting, drug and alcohol abuse, and suicide can be the results of turning anger inward. Sometimes, when anger controls thoughts and emotions, an individual needs the help and support of a qualified counselor.

## Imputing Motives

It is difficult enough to be objective when you have been offended. It is impossible to be objective if you don't investigate the real motives of the offender. Imputing a wrong motive can lead to disastrous conclusions.

After my wife and I were married for a few years, she approached me with a revelation. She said that there were times in our marriage when she had wondered why I was treating her with deliberate meanness. She had come to the realization that most of the time I was unaware of the hurt I was causing. When she understood my real motive (in this case ignorance), she didn't feel as hurt by my actions. In many cases, all she had to do was communicate the effects of my hurtful actions and the conflict was on the road to being resolved.

Asking an offender why he did what he did, and listening to his answers without preconceived conclusions, can go a long way to avoiding conflicts that are simply based on misunderstandings.

## Allowing Yourself to Become Bitter

"Pursue peace with all people, and holiness, without which no one will see the Lord: looking carefully lest anyone fall short of the grace of God; lest any root of bitterness springing up cause trouble; and by this many become defiled" (Hebrews 12:14-15).

A tree can suffer a great deal of damage to its branches or leaves and still survive. The root system is what keeps the tree stable. When roots become diseased a tree may appear healthy for a while. If the disease isn't treated, in time the entire tree becomes infected and dies. In the same way, emotional bitterness eats away at the very roots of our emotions and thoughts until it affects all the branches of our lives.

Bitterness is a state of mind built on unresolved anger. Bitterness creates a hardened heart, making it difficult for you to respond to God or to forgive an offender. An attitude of bitterness can begin in any area of life. It can start as unhappiness with your job. It can begin as a sense of frustration in unfulfilled dreams. It can be planted when you are offended. No matter how it begins, once established, bitterness takes control of your life.

**Example:** A husband and wife can't solve the disagreements between them. They are ashamed to seek help. Yelling, ignoring each other and abusing one another emotionally become a way of life. In time the wife can't see any good in her husband, but dwells only on his negative qualities. Her husband has less and less value in her eyes. Eventually, she comes to despise the marriage covenant they made with God. She knows that in Mark 10 Jesus teaches that divorce is against the will of God, but motivated by bitterness, she refuses to take the matter to God and to seek his ways. Finally, she convinces herself that since God loves her and wants her to be happy, God actually wants her to divorce her husband.

**Example:** A man becomes frustrated because his career didn't turn out the way he planned. He wants a better house, another car, more recognition. The frustration grows into anger and he becomes obsessed with the "success" of others. He begins to see obedience to God's laws as holding him back from what he really deserves. Since he can't justify anger against God, he begins to express anger against church leaders because in his mind they're the ones who make him obey God. He scrutinizes everything they do and exposes their faults to anyone who will listen. Because of his discontent, he is in constant conflict with leaders and members of the congregation. Eventually, he decides that all organized religion is hypocrisy. He now feels free to disobey biblical instructions while claiming to be more "spiritual."

**Example:** A woman loses her temper and mistreats a friend in public. The mistreated friend is confused and hurt. She goes to the offender, but the woman replies, "Don't pretend you don't know what you did." The woman who is mistreated can't figure out why her friend is upset and she becomes angry and bitter. She shares this incident with all of her friends. They take her side, shunning the offender. The offender does the same with her friends. Soon there are two groups, both claiming the other is mean-spirited, squared off against each other in a war of gossip and slander.

Bitterness, once rooted in your emotional processes, begins to feed every aspect of your life with emotional poison. You avoid bitterness by refusing to obsess over the hurts and injustices of life and by deciding to appreciate the goodness of God and his blessings. When you obsess over an offense, you rob yourself of happiness.

Have you ever thought about what would make you truly happy—a new car, a change in your job, a new husband or wife, more money, or better looks? Maybe your definition of happiness is to find a special someone, to get married and to have children. Maybe your definition of happiness is to become a doctor, helping others; or perhaps to become an entrepreneur, being your own boss.

Now imagine what it would be like to have everything you think would make you happy, but then suddenly losing it all. That's exactly what happened to Viktor Frankl.

Viktor Frankl was one of the most promising and well-known Austrian psychiatrists in the 1930s. He was highly successful, happily married and admired by colleagues. One day his entire life came crashing down as he and his wife found themselves violently removed from their home, robbed of everything they owned, and crammed into a boxcar bound for a Nazi concentration camp. Once they arrived, Viktor was separated from his wife, whom he would never see again. He was stripped of his clothes, his head was shaved and his personal identity reduced to a number tattooed on his arm.

Frankl would spend the next few years living in indescribable horror. He slept with nine other men in a bed only six-to-eight feet wide with no mattress and only two blankets. He received so little food that his body soon looked like skin stretched over a skeleton. He endured brutal beatings from Nazi guards and fellow prisoners. He watched countless people suffer and die. In the midst of the most unimaginable horror, Viktor Frankl discovered one of the most important keys to happiness.

The famous psychiatrist had written down his life's work into a book and sewn it into his coat. When the Germans took his coat, he was required to wear the rags of an inmate who had been gassed. Frankl was devastated. He had already lost his family, wealth and prestige, but now he had also lost the summation of his life's work. His life was stripped of its meaning and with it any hope for happiness. It was then that he reached into the pocket of this tattered coat and found a page from a Jewish prayer book. After the war, Frankl would write about how reading this prayer was a profound crossroads in his life: "How should I have interpreted such a 'coincidence' other than a challenge to live my thoughts instead of merely putting them on paper?" (*Man's Search for Meaning*, Victor E. Frankl, Beacon Press, 1992, pp. 118-119.)

Frankl began to look for a greater meaning for human life. The search for a higher meaning allowed Frankl to discover God's love and involvement, even in the midst of the unspeakable horrors of Auschwitz. He actually was able to choose not to be bitter in the most abusive situation imaginable.

This doesn't mean that Frankl concluded that the Nazis should escape justice for their monstrous crimes. It did mean that in spite of his horrendous experiences, he refused to become filled with hatred and bitterness and obsessed with vengeance.

You were created in the image of God with the purpose to be his child. Why waste your life consumed with bitterness toward another human being? Every day, even a day when you are faced with hurt and abuse, is an opportunity to experience God's purpose for you in recreating your corrupt human nature into the character of one of his children.

## Involving Others in Your Discontent

One of the most difficult behaviors to control when you have been offended is the desire to share your discontent with others. When struggling with the emotions of betrayal, you often need to confide in a close friend or a trusted counselor who can help you sort through potential responses, decide on right actions and avoid bitterness. Involving others for this reason is often necessary for us to find objectivity.

A problem arises when you feel a need to share your story with anyone who will listen as you defame the offending person, hoping to gather allies in the process. The Bible uses a colorful word to describe the tearing down of another's character. That word is "backbiting," which appears in Proverbs 25:23: "The north wind brings rain, and a backbiting tongue an angry countenance."

There are times when a person's sins should be shared with others. A good example is when family and friends get together for an intervention with an alcoholic. The public apology of a political or church leader who has acted inappropriately is an example of when it may be suitable to share a person's sins with a number of people. These actions, however, must be done in the context of strict guidelines.

Absalom shared his hurt and discontent with others until he formed a political party big enough to try overthrowing his father's kingdom. Gathering friends and relatives to your side like a lynch mob can be nothing more than a way of spreading your bitterness to others. In doing so, you mistake vengeance for justice.

Paul tells the Ephesians:

"Do not let any unwholesome talk come out of your mouths, but only what is helpful for building others up according to their needs, that it may benefit those who listen.... Get rid of all bitterness, rage and anger, brawling and slander, along with every form of malice. Be kind and compassionate to one another, forgiving one another, just as in Christ God forgave you" (Ephesians 4:29, 31-32 NIV).

An irony of obsession is that by concentrating on the behavior of the abuser, a person may in turn become an abuser. We strike back by verbally attacking the abuser's reputation in bitterness and malice. Our behavior can end up as morally wrong, or even worse, than the behavior of the person who committed the offense against us.

## Viewing Life as a Victim

A frustrating aspect of life is that we have so little control over many of the bad things that happen to us. As mentioned earlier, this is one of the reasons why we feel a need to control others. We can't control our genetics, where we were born or the weather. We have no control over the drunk driver who swerves into our car, nor can we change the fact that there is no cure for the common cold. Many things that happen to us are unfair. We may be fired because the boss wants to hire his nephew. The transmission goes out in the car and we don't have the money to fix it. The church choir director seems to pick on us at every practice even though we practice our part.

When we view life as victims, we see all of our troubles as the result of another person's abuse. The truth is, everyone is a victim in one way or another. Some people seem to go through life with little abuse or difficulties. Others seem doomed by horrible misuse, poverty and violence. The only control we have over these problems is how we respond to them. We either choose to find God's purpose in our suffering, or we choose to respond as helpless victims.

Viewing life as a victim keeps you from taking responsibility for your actions, and makes it almost impossible for you to experience healthy relationships with other people. When you automatically expect others to hurt you, every relationship will self-destruct.

In his book *Happiness is a Serious Problem*, Dennis Prager gives five reasons why seeing life as a victim is appealing (Regan Books, 1998, pp. 83-86):

- It is easier to blame others than to confront life and oneself.

- Victims get sympathy.

- It is easier not to take control of your life.

- Self-pity is addictive.

- It is hard to mature.

Interestingly, all five of these points describe the path of least resistance, allowing us to defend our corrupt human nature. This isn't to imply that people aren't real victims of terrible crimes or hurtful abuse. When we suffer from abuse, we need healing, comfort and understanding. We need to believe that there can still be goodness in life. The challenge is how to endure and to heal from those events so that God can create goodness in our lives.

The problem with adopting a victim mentality is that you create a personal story of being victimized, even when faced with the normal inconsistencies and unfairness of everyday life. Everyone isn't always trying to get you. Bad things don't always occur because someone planned to hurt you. Many things that happen to you in life are a result of everyone else being just as confused, dysfunctional and out of touch with God as you are. We must learn not to take everything so personally.

Now you can see why we started with a message to the injured person. Only after receiving help from God: do you have the power to offer forgiveness; are you able to realize that it's not always about winning; can you become dedicated to seeking God's solution instead of trying to make the offender meet your expectations; and can you constructively deal with your anger and bitterness.

Now let's look at the biblical instructions concerning the person who committed the offense.

# 5

# The Healing Process: Message to the Offender

But whoever causes one of these little ones who believes in Me to sin, it would be better for him if a millstone were hung around his neck, and he were drowned in the depth of the sea. Woe to the world because of offenses! For offenses must come, but woe to that man by whom the offenses come! (Matthew 18:6-7).

Those are strong words from Jesus to those who cause another person to sin. What is required of us if our offensive behavior influences someone else to sin through bitterness or hatred? What is required of us when we have sinned against a fellow Christian? What kind of confession or restitution is necessary? How should a Christian respond to the accusation that he or she has sinned against a brother or sister?

The answers to these questions are found by dealing with the same five motivations we addressed in previous chapters. Those desires cause all human conflict.

## Solution #1: First Seek to be Reconciled to God

When we are reconciled to God there is little wiggle room for self-justification. God sets the standards and we must take responsibility for our actions.

There are three kinds of consequences we suffer because of sin. One is the natural consequences in this life. A person may get drunk and have a car accident that leaves him paralyzed. This is the natural result of sin.

The second is a temporary punishment from God. God may expose your dishonesty so that you are fired from a job in order to teach a lesson. The book of Hebrews instructs us about God's chastening:

> If you endure chastening, God deals with you as with sons; for what son is there whom a father does not chasten? But if you are without chastening, of which all have become partakers, then you are illegitimate and not sons. Furthermore, we have had human fathers who corrected us, and we paid them respect. Shall we not much more readily be in subjection to the Father of spirits and live? For they indeed for a few days chastened us as seemed best to them, but He for our profit, that we may be partakers of His holiness. Now no chastening seems to be joyful for the present, but painful; nevertheless, afterward it yields the peaceable fruit of righteousness to those who have been trained by it (Hebrews 12:7-11).

God's temporary punishment is for our own good—like a parent punishing a child to teach her not to play in the street. God's forgiveness doesn't always erase the natural consequences or temporary punishment.

The third result of sin is eternal. The ministry of reconciliation is about how God pardons sins and expunges the eternal consequences.

When you realize that you have sinned against someone, you must first recognize that you have also sinned against God. This means taking responsibility by going to God and repenting; confessing and making restitution to the offended person; and accepting the temporary consequences for your wrongdoing. William Bennett, in *The Book of Virtues*, has this to say about responsibility:

> To 'respond' is to 'answer.' Correspondingly, to be 'responsible' is to be 'answerable,' to be accountable. Irresponsible behavior is immature behavior. Taking responsibility–being responsible–is a sign of maturity....
>
> In the end we are answerable for the kinds of persons we have made of ourselves. 'That's just the way I am!' is not an excuse for inconsiderate or vile behavior. Nor is it even an accurate description, for we are never just what we are.... we become what we are as persons by the decisions that we ourselves make....
>
> A weakened sense of responsibility does not weaken the fact of responsibility.
>
> Responsible persons are mature people who have taken charge of themselves and their conduct, who own their actions and own up to them—who answer for them (Simon and Schuster, 1993, pp. 185-6).

A sense of responsibility, based on the acknowledgement that we are reconciled to God through the terrible sacrifice of his Son, requires us to be reconciled to our brother if we have sinned against him. Jesus taught in the Sermon on the Mount that we should reconcile with a brother whom we have offended before bringing a gift of worship to God.

> If you bring your gift to the altar, and there remember that your brother has something against you, leave your gift before the altar, and go your way. First be reconciled to your brother, and then come and offer your gift (Matthew 5:23-24).

When we are acutely aware of our reconciliation with God, we become sensitive to our need to reconcile with those whom we have offended. We must also recognize that because all sin is against God, the act of mistreating others erects a barrier between us and God. Peter pointed out this principle when he wrote to Christian husbands to honor their wives "that your prayers may not be hindered" (1 Peter 3:7).

When we refuse to repent and reconcile with our brothers or sisters, we find ourselves in conflict with our Creator. This is why repentance toward God is part of the process of being reconciled to a fellow Christian.

## Solution #2: Seek Humility

"By pride comes nothing but strife" (Proverbs 13:10).

Possibly the most difficult aspect of repenting is dealing with pride. It is hard to see ourselves as wrong. When we do accept that we are wrong, we tend to justify ourselves by claiming that someone else caused us to do it.

In Genesis 3 we see that when humanity's parents chose to eat of the tree of the knowledge of good and evil there was an immediate change in their nature. Before their decision to assume God's prerogative to determine right from wrong, there was no shame in the sexual differences between husband and wife. After eating the fruit, they felt shame because of their "nakedness."

They then hid themselves from God. Guilt was also a new experience for them. They were designed to experience a relationship with their Creator. Now they experienced intense internal conflict as they were driven by their corrupted nature to hide from his presence.

When confronted with his sin, Adam blamed "[the] woman whom You gave to be with me, she gave me of the tree, and I ate." For the first time Adam found himself having to defend his corrupted image. He not only blamed his wife for causing him to sin, but subtly blamed God since it was he who made the woman. Eve blamed Satan, although she was a little more honest when she admitted to being deceived (Genesis 3:6-13).

It is difficult for us to admit wrong because we see ourselves as little gods who determine what is right and wrong. Like Adam, we have a strong desire to defend our self-made image.

Dale Carnegie in *How to Win Friends and Influence People* captures the defensive side of human nature in the account of a gangster named "Two Gun" Crowley. Crowley was a Depression Era desperado who killed without conscience. On May 7, 1931 the police had the famous criminal holed up in a New York City apartment. After a vicious gun battle a wounded Crowley was hauled away by the authorities. They found a note he had scrawled during the shootout. It read, in part, "Under my coat is a weary heart, but a kind one–one that would do nobody any harm."

Before the shootout a policeman had walked up on "Two Gun" and his girlfriend in a parked car. Crowley had gunned down the officer in a barrage of gunfire. Carnegie tells of the murderer's fate:

> Crowley was sentenced to the electric chair. When he arrived in the death house in Sing Sing, did he say, "This is what I get for killing people?" No, he said, "This is what I get for defending myself."

> The point of the story is this: "Two Gun" Crowley didn't blame himself for anything (Simon and Schuster, 1964, pp. 19-20).

In some ways Crowley's exaggerated view of himself isn't any different from the way the rest of us tend to see ourselves. Pride makes it difficult to admit even the smallest of mistakes.

The opposite of pride is humility. Humility begins with heart-felt recognition of your own spiritual poverty before God, followed by admitting your natural hostility toward him, confessing your disobedience to his law, and wanting a change in your nature. It is only through Christ's crossing of the impassable chasm that we can be reconciled to God. He did this while you and I were his enemies. This understanding of God's love motivates us to accept the ugliness of our sins, to seek God's forgiveness, and then to seek the forgiveness of those whom we have sinned against.

Paul told the Philippians:

> Let nothing be done through selfish ambition or conceit, but in lowliness of mind let each esteem others better than himself. Let each of you look out not only for his own interests, but also for the interests of others (Philippians 2:3-4).

Paul gives us important keys to analyzing our own motivations when confronted by someone whom we've offended. Here are some questions you need to ask yourself when feeling resistance towards someone who has come to you concerning an offense:

- Am I resisting taking responsibility for my actions because of a need to appear righteous? Do I feel that confessing will make others lose respect for me?

- Am I resisting taking responsibility for my actions because I see the other person as spiritually inferior to me? Do I accept this imperfect brother or sister as an equal child of God? (Matthew 18:10-14).

- Am I willing to listen to the offended person and to strive to understand his or her viewpoint?

- Am I willing to take the offended person's interests as seriously as my own interests?

(For a more complete self-evaluation, see *The Peacemaker* by Ken Sande, Baker Books, 2004.)

Continuing in Philippians 2, Paul gives Christians an example of humility to emulate:

> Your attitude should be the same as that of Jesus Christ: who, being in very nature God, did not consider equality with God something to be grasped, but made himself nothing, taking the very nature of a servant, being made in human likeness. And being found in appearance as a man, he humbled himself and became obedient to death— even death on a cross! (Philippians 2:5-8 NIV).

Humility and spiritual poverty before God are the keys to reconciliation for both the offended person and the one who committed the offense. Only after both parties understand the ministry of reconciliation between them and God can they begin to apply the biblical instructions for reconciliation between Christians.

## Solution #3: Give Up Your Need to Control the Response of the Other Person

Remember, the natural reaction of corrupt human nature is to protect our rights, self-image and emotional security. Even when we admit to wrongdoing, we generally want to control the actions of the person who is confronting us. The natural comeback to being shown error is something like, "Okay, I was wrong, but you have a problem because you shouldn't be so angry with me."

When we are shown that we are wrong, our initial reaction to the offended person should be to acknowledge the offense and to ask for forgiveness. If we have hurt someone through action or misunderstanding, or even through ignorance, we should be willing to confess any wrong that has contributed to the conflict.

Confession is more than simply saying, "I'm sorry." To confess is to spell out your wrongdoing clearly so that the offended person sees that you understand, and that you take responsibility. This type of confession includes explaining your motivation or ignorance of the effects of your actions. You need to confess your wrongdoing and receive forgiveness before pointing out to the accuser how he may have contributed to the problem.

Taking responsibility also means being willing to make restitution (Exodus 21-22). If you have damaged another person's property, you must be willing to pay for the damage. When you have slandered someone, you must be willing to set the record straight.

> **Example:** Your mutt digs under the fence, and then impregnates the neighbor's prize, thoroughbred poodle. You apologize, fill in the hole under the fence and chain your dog up at night. These are proper actions, but it still isn't restitution. Restitution means you must also be willing to pay costs for the poodle, which is no longer suitable for breeding. Forgiveness doesn't mean the damaged person is required to forgo restitution.

Slandering and gossip are more difficult to remedy. It is amazing how easy it is for people to viciously attack other people on social media by writing things they would never say to those people face-to-face. If you find that you have posted something untrue about someone, then you have a moral responsibility to make an apology on the same site. Even after you make an apology, the person you slandered may never regain trust and appreciation from others because of a damaged reputation.

You can't minimize your sin by being upset because the other person is offended. Trying to control the reactions of the offended person will only lead to more offense. (Ordering the offended person to "calm down" only throws fuel on the fire.) When confronted by someone whom you have offended, you must analyze your contribution to the conflict, confess your involvement and offer to make restitution.

## Solution #4: Seek God's Solution Instead of Fulfilling Your Desires and Expectations

When confronted with a person you've offended, take time to listen to the complaint. Resist the need to explain your side of the story immediately. Ask questions to help clarify the person's reasons and feelings. If you find yourself responding in anger, ask for a few minutes to think about what he or she has said. Here are some questions you need to ask yourself:

- Did I sin against this person or hurt him or her through fault or ignorance. Or has there been some kind of miscommunication between us? How did I contribute?

- How must I take responsibility for my actions? How must I confess and make restitution?

- What lessons can God teach me through this situation?

- Am I being defensive because I feel threatened?

- Am I angry because my pride is injured?

(For a more complete self-evaluation, see *The Peacemaker* by Ken Sande, Baker Books, 2004.)

The relationship may not be restored immediately just because you take responsibility and ask forgiveness. It takes time for emotional wounds to heal. Trust is earned. Once broken, it may take time and effort to rebuild.

Proverbs tells us: "A brother offended is harder to win than a strong city, and contentions are like the bars of a castle" (Proverbs 18:19).

When you are the offender, you should strive to help that person heal through intercessory prayer, understanding, confession and patience.

## Solution #5:
## Seek to Avoid Damaging the Emotions of Others

Jesus offended many people during his ministry. Those offenses weren't due to meanness or egocentricities. He did not feel a need to project his rights onto others, nor did he manipulate people to meet his expectations. People were offended by Jesus because he taught the truth of God. There are times when the truth strikes at the core of our corrupted human nature. We don't want to see ourselves as a mangled image of God, so we defend the false images we've created. This is true for both the offender and the person who is offended.

Although Jesus may have offended people with the truth, he was always careful not to offend others needlessly. He and Peter were discussing the fairness of the Messiah having to pay the temple tax. At the end of the discussion Jesus told Peter to pay the tax "lest we offend them" (Matthew 17:24-27). Jesus was "greater than the temple," yet he avoided pointless conflict. Christians should avoid causing unnecessary offenses.

Christians should never shy away from presenting the truth of God, but we should also reflect the Christ-like behavior of peacemakers. I've heard people say that they believe in being "brutally honest." Most people with this approach to conflict tend to be more brutal than honest.

As offenders, we are required to reach out to help heal other people. This includes praying for the emotional and spiritual healing of the person offended. Seeking forgiveness and making restitution for doing someone harm takes a great sense of responsibility and love. If we are reconciled to God through the work of Jesus Christ, what choice do we have but to seek to be reconciled to those whom we have wronged?

We can now take a look at various levels and intensity of conflict, as well as some principles of conflict resolution.

# 6

# Dealing with the Five Levels of Conflict

The natural inclination of broken human beings is to be at war with God and each other. To reconcile with God we must understand and deal with the root causes of conflict within ourselves. (We'll cover this in the next chapter.) Then we can learn how to manage conflict with others.

So far we've looked at what both the offended and the offender need to do to be reconciled to God before they approach resolving conflict with each other. If we've reconciled to God, why isn't conflict management now just a matter of sitting down and solving the problems?

We tend to invest little emotional energy into a minor disagreement or misunderstanding, quickly forgetting it. When a disagreement involves major decisions, emotional or physical security, core values, or a sense of self-worth, we tend to invest a lot of emotional energy. The more emotional energy we invest, the more intense the conflict. As we devote more and more energy to a problem, disagreements and misunderstandings escalate into arguments, contests, damaged relationships, and eventually, even hatred and bitterness.

It's obvious that there are different levels of conflict. Kenneth C. Haugk in *Antagonist in the Church* pinpoints five levels of conflict. Let's take a look at each of these five levels. Then we'll look at some basic principles of conflict management to bring about constructive solutions. Remember, on a spiritual level we can successfully apply principles of conflict management only after we have dealt with the five major motivations and desires within us that cause conflict.

1.  **Problems to Solve.** At this level of conflict the focus is on a problem and the common goal is finding a solution. The people involved may have different ideas and may express those ideas passionately. Discussions are open and language tends to be directed at the problem, not at other people. There are no hidden personal agendas. All parties are motivated to maintain unity, create consensus and find a solution.

These kinds of conflicts happen every day and can lead to productive problem solving as long as the parties are willing to stay focused on the problem and to continue finding solutions. Brainstorming, allowing everyone to contribute, and a willingness to sacrifice personal goals for common goals creates teamwork and consensus. When conflict is managed at this level, the parties tend to produce win-win solutions.

> **Example:** A husband and wife are considering moving to a bigger house. They look at a dozen houses, analyze the options, make adjustments to their budget and the reality of the market, and decide on what features are necessary and which ones are not as important. In the end they come to a decision that is a win-win for both parties.

2.  **Disagreements.** At this level the discussions become more emotional as the emphasis is more on differences than solutions. People tend to be self-protective, sometimes making comments directed at other people instead of the problem. At this level of conflict, compromise becomes the common method

of resolution. Compromise can be a good solution unless it leaves one or more parties feeling exploited or neglected.

> **Example:** Let's look at the same couple who are considering moving into a bigger house. They narrow their choices down to one house. One of the attractive features is a large bonus room. The problem is that the man wants to make the bonus room into his "man cave" while the woman wants to use it as a space where she can enjoy her hobby of quilt making. They must seek a compromise, but when both parties care for the welfare of the other, a solution will be reached without any rancor or long term disappointment.

When we are focused on disagreements we can lose emotional perspective. Instead of looking for common solutions, we feel a need to defend our ideas or self-image. There are three actions we can take to help move this level of conflict back into problem-solving mode.

First, we can analyze our own emotions to see whether we are contributing to the conflict by being defensive. Sometimes this means taking time out to calm down and to think through not only the problem but our reaction.

Second, take time to analyze the situation to see whether we truly understand the other person's ideas, or we have simply discounted those ideas without due consideration. A proverb states, "He who answers a matter before he hears it, It is folly and shame to him" (Proverbs 18:13).

This means actively listening to the other person. Many times when another person is talking you might be only half listening because you are formulating your response. Have you ever found yourself wishing someone would finish a story because you have a bigger and better one to tell?

Active listening takes a lot of self-discipline. It means concentrating on what the other person is saying with the intent of understanding his or her viewpoint. The real test of active listening is whether you are able to repeat the other person's view after he or she is finished talking. If the other person says, "That is not what I meant," you must ask questions and listen to the responses until you can correctly state the other person's views. This doesn't mean you agree with that individual (although once you can repeat back his or her views, you may find some agreement). It does mean that you understand.

Through active listening you can explore and emphasize areas of agreement before moving to areas of disagreement. This is important because it is easier to build a consensus by first focusing on areas of agreement. Sometimes it is good to write down and read out loud the areas of agreement before writing down and defining the areas of disagreement.

As strife degenerates into more dysfunctional levels of conflict, understanding and trust between the parties deteriorates. We'll discuss trust a little later in this chapter.

3. **Contests.** Conflict at this point is a win / lose proposition in which each party is bent on showing that the other person or group is wrong. Even so, people who are committed to a common vision and mission can sometimes still arrive at healthy resolutions in contest mode, although at times individuals are left hurt and angry.

**Example:** Our couple have two different visions of the perfect house. He wants a big screen TV and leather furniture in the living room where he can watch sports with his friends. She wants the living room to be furnished with formal furniture, paintings and decorative curios. Both feel that they will be unhappy if they don't get what they want. What ensues is a contest of wills. They accuse each other of being selfish and unreasonable. Whatever compromise is produced leaves one, or both, of them feeling like they were cheated.

Here are a few approaches to consider when conflict degenerates into a contest. First, take time to seek humility before God. At the contest stage, pride can be a major motivation. Second, when a person's actions are unprincipled or unlawful, then it may be impossible to find a solution.

Third, sometimes a boss or a parent might have to take a stance that literally forces the other person into compliance. Unless the parties have good emotional rapport, this mode of dealing with conflict will eventually create an adversarial relationship.

Fourth, you must be willing to seek compromise in areas where compromise is appropriate. This doesn't mean you compromise with biblical principles! However, in order to solve personal conflicts at the contest level, all of us must compromise with personal preferences and desires. Otherwise, we will be constantly engaged in a contest of wills. Solomon tells us, "When a man's ways please the LORD, He makes even his enemies to be at peace with him" (Proverbs 16:7).

We all have to accept the concept that teamwork requires sacrifices on the part of each team member. When we must compromise, we must do so without holding a grudge. If you find yourself always defending your honor or believing that only unprincipled people compromise, then you don't understand the nature of teamwork.

I want to reiterate that willingness to compromise with a personal idea or method for the sake of teamwork doesn't mean compromising on biblical principle. Intellectual honesty is absolutely necessary at this point. We must be biblically educated and emotionally willing to analyze the difference between biblical principle and personal opinion.

Sometimes, at this stage of conflict, a mediator is needed. Before you engage a mediator, carefully and objectively re-examine your position. Consider that you may be at least partially wrong. It is best to work out conflict before you involve a mediator because you may find out that the ruling goes against your position and your reputation is harmed. Solomon reminds us:

Do not go hastily to court; For what will you do in the end, When your neighbor has put you to shame? Debate your case with your neighbor, And do not disclose the secret to another; Lest he who hears it expose your shame, And your reputation be ruined (Proverbs 25:8-10).

4. **Fight or Flight.** At this stage of conflict, objectivity becomes difficult because one party, or both, are emotionally invested in the conflict to the point that they feel compelled to defeat the other person or simply to run away from the situation.

**Example:** The house hunting couple have many unresolved conflicts in their relationship. Because they both lack trust and harbor deep animosity towards each other, they have an automatic negative reaction to each other when they have different opinions. Even the smallest issues ignite a defensive and angry reaction. One of them may decide that the best thing to do is to withdraw from the idea of a new house and to refuse to cooperate with the other person. The fight over the new house is the symptom of a relationship defined by unresolved conflict.

When a conflict has risen in intensity to *fight or flight* status, it is probably best for everyone involved to take some time out to search for spiritual, mental and emotional perspective. It is not a sign of weakness to tell someone that you're upset and need some time to think through the situation.

It is also important to consider that in *fight or flight* mode it is not always possible to deal with the original problem until hurt emotions are discussed and trust is reestablished.

5. **Antagonism.** An antagonist sees the other person as an adversary who must be punished or controlled in spite of the cost to self or others.

Christians should want to live peaceably with all people and to be able to resolve conflict. Unfortunately, there are certain people who are so set in their ways that it is impossible to resolve conflict with them unless you allow them to dominate the relationship.

> **Example:** The husband of our house hunters is filled with anger towards his wife. He constantly puts her down and tries to make her feel unworthy. He tries to dominate every decision.

Antagonists thrive on unhealthy conflict. They believe that they are superior to others. They also possess deep-seated hatred for authority and the overwhelming need to control. They are constantly critical. Sometimes they can be angry and in-your-face. At other times antagonists can be manipulative, even seeming to support you (until things are done in ways they don't like).

The book of Proverbs describes this kind of person:

> A scoundrel plots evil, and his speech is like a scorching fire. A perverse man stirs up dissension, and a gossip separates close friends. A violent man entices his neighbor and leads him down a path that is not good. He who winks with his eye is plotting perversity; he who purses his lips is bent on evil (Proverbs 16:27-30, NIV).

An antagonist's desire for control creates no-win situations. Sometimes you have to confront an antagonist head-on. Be careful how and when you do, however, because this type of person loves to break down the credibility of anyone who confronts him or her. If you are a manager, sometimes you have to "marginalize" the antagonist by building relationships with those under his sway until he no longer has any real influence.

The hard reality is that it is impossible to build a healthy relationship with an antagonist until that person finds peace with God.

## Principles of Conflict Management

Now we can begin to explore some basic principles of conflict resolution.

**1.  Before approaching an individual, review the major factors that motivate conflict and explore your spiritual and emotional stability.**

Here are the five major motivational factors in conflict we discussed in previous chapters.

---

### Five Major Factors that Motivate Conflict

1.  Corrupt human nature, which leads to conflict with God.

2.  Pride—an exaggerated view of self-importance.

3.  The need to control other people's responses.

4.  Unrealistic expectations that others will satisfy all of our needs and desires.

5.  The need for emotional healing.

---

**2.  When you have to confront someone, pick the time, the place and the choice of words carefully.**

Once an argument begins, it tends to escalate quickly into

anger and irrational behavior. It is much better to deal with the issues while both parties are calm. It is important to pick the proper time and place for discussion. If emotions are beginning to run high, ask for a short break to get control. Once a person is offended or hurt, you'll need much more effort and time to come to a resolution.

Solomon tells us "The beginning of strife is like releasing water; Therefore stop contention before a quarrel starts" (Proverbs 17:14) and "A brother offended is harder to win than a strong city, and contentions are like the bars of a castle" (Proverbs 18:19).

One of the greatest examples of carefully dealing with serious conflict by picking the time, the place and the choice of words is found in the biblical story of Queen Esther.

Forced to marry a Persian king who had absolute power, she made the best of the situation. When a plot to destroy the Jews was uncovered, she risked her life to save her people. She had to confront her husband with the fact that his top aide, Haman, was plotting genocide against the Jews.

Esther took great risks to do what was right. First of all, there was great risk because no one could come before the king unless he granted permission. Second, Esther would have to reveal herself as Jewish, thereby risking extinction with her people. Through her grace and tact, God saved His people (Esther 4:13-16; 5:1-7:10).

**3. Strive to make the other person know you care about him or her as an individual in spite of the disagreement or misunderstanding.**

It is important to express disagreement while maintaining the value of the relationship. Before reacting in anger, think about the importance of the relationship to you and the damage you may do to the other person. Even when confronted with an unresolvable conflict, a person who is reconciled to God will strive to reflect that relationship to the other person.

There may be times when a relationship, such as one with a manipulative and uncooperative co-worker, can't be salvaged. At those times you may simply have to walk away from the situation, giving up on resolving the conflict.

**4. Seek to understand the issue from the other person's viewpoint before proving your point.**

You seldom convince a person to accept your side until you can define that individual's viewpoint and understand why he or she has taken a position.

Stephen Covey wrote in *Principle Centered Leadership*:

Perhaps the most powerful principle of all human interaction: genuinely seeking to understand another deeply before being understood in return. At the root of all interpersonal problems is a failure to thoroughly understand each other. The actual disagreements of substance are magnified and compounded by our inability to see the world not only through another's eyes, but also through his or her mind and heart. We misunderstand and therefore mistrust motives, points of view—we are so ego-invested in advancing our own ideas, defending our position, attacking contrary opinion, judging, evaluating, probing and questioning—that we normally listen with the intent not to understand but to respond (*Principle Centered Leadership*, Stephen Covey, Summit Books, 1991 p. 272.)

We're back to the importance of active listening. Active listening means to concentrate, not on your reply, but on what the person is really saying. It means asking questions and clarifying the other person's position. This can be difficult; especially when you know the other person is wrong or is being accusatory. By asking the right questions, though, you can sometimes get the person to find the solution on his or her own, thus transforming the conflict into productive negotiation.

### 5.  Praise before you criticize.

This doesn't mean that we should use vain flattery or try to deceive others by "buttering them up." It means that we should allow people a chance to back out of conflict by emphasizing their good points and contributions. We need to allow people the chance to say "I'm sorry."

Appeal to good motives. It is much more effective to say, "Honey, I know this is a sacrifice for you, but I really need you to help me move some things into the garage" than, "You're so lazy. You never help me out around here. I've been after you to help me move those boxes into the garage for two weeks."

### 6.  Seek to create solutions in which everyone benefits.

In *The Seven Habits of Highly Effective People* Stephen Covey calls these "win-win" solutions. Effective conflict resolution means working with people to create new solutions that benefit all individuals involved.

Many times we look at a problem and think there is only one solution. Famous psychologist Abraham Maslow once said, "People who are only good with hammers see every problem as a nail." Just because a solution worked in one situation doesn't mean it will work in the next.

During the early stages of World War II the Japanese experienced a number of stunning victories in China, Asia and the South Pacific. Convinced that they were invincible, the Japanese continued to expand their empire until they overextended their resources and logistical system. Faced with overwhelming Allied power, the Japanese failed to adapt. The result was defeat after bloody defeat. The Japanese coined a word for the arrogance and rigid thinking that led to their inability to consider new methods.

It is translated into English as "victory disease."

In your life, when the methods of past success are not working, the answer isn't in doggedly pursuing failing solutions.

Brainstorming is a method of first considering all possible solutions to a problem, and then objectively sorting through the ideas. Have participants write down their ideas before the meeting. (There is a proclivity to concentrate on the first solutions mentioned. If people have written down their ideas, then the moderator can ask each one to read his or her suggestions.) Then write down and display possible solutions, listing the potential good results and bad results of each decision. This way you will be better able to sort out the various ideas and to find ones that offer the best solutions.

7.   **Practice the art of the "soft answer.**

"A soft answer turns away wrath, But a harsh word stirs up anger" (Proverbs 15:1).

There is a well-known story about educator Booker T. Washington. Not long after he became president of Tuskegee Institute in Alabama, Washington was walking in an exclusive part of town when a white woman asked if he would like to make some money chopping wood. Washington took on the chore, chopped the wood and carried it into the house. It was there that the woman's daughter recognized him. The next day the embarrassed woman showed up at his office to apologize.

Washington is reported to have replied that he enjoyed doing manual labor and doing favors for friends. His humility and soft answer impressed the woman so much that she became instrumental in raising thousands of dollars for Tuskegee Institute.

Sometimes conflict requires a harsh answer, but how many conflicts can be steered in a different direction with some humility and a soft answer?

### 8.  Some issues aren't worth fighting over.

In the book of Genesis we see that Abraham was willing to allow Lot to choose what seemed to be the best land in order to keep peace. This was an honest expression on Abraham's part. He didn't allow Lot to choose while secretly feeling cheated by his nephew (Genesis 13:1-12). Abraham was careful to select which hills on which he was willing to fight and die.

It is a wise proverb that states, "It is honorable for a man to stop striving, since any fool can start a quarrel" (Proverbs 20:3).

### 9.  Peacemaking isn't appeasement.

It is important to remember that peacemaking isn't appeasement. In Aesop's Fables there is the story of a middle-aged man who married two wives. One was a middle-aged woman who wanted him to look older. The other wife was a much younger woman who wanted her husband to look more her age. Every day the older woman pulled out one of the man's dark hairs to make him look older while the younger woman worked on pulling out his gray hairs to make him look younger. He enjoyed their attention, until one day he woke up completely bald.

The moral of the story is that when you try to please everyone, you end up pleasing no one. Loving others means that their happiness is important to you, but it is wrong to enable a person to take advantage of your love. You may actually be hurting a loved one by allowing him or her to be demanding and selfish.

## The Issue of Trust

It seems that many times people tend to fall into two categories: those gullible souls who trust everyone and the cynics who trust no one.

The basis of all relationships is trust. Stephen M.R. Covey gives this definition of trust in his book *The Speed of Trust*: "Simply put, trust means *confidence*. The opposite of trust—distrust—is *suspicion*" (Free Press, 2006, p, 5). *Webster's Dictionary* defines trust as "assured reliance on the character, ability, strength or truth of someone or something."

No relationship can be healthy if one or both parties are constantly suspicious of the other party. The more suspicious you are of someone, the more you discount that individual's actions and doubt his or her motives. Of course, conflict erodes trust.

Before we deal with trust issues between individuals, let's first explore trusting in God. Having confidence in God's honesty, reliability, integrity and goodness gives us the ability to apply his solutions to relationship problems.

Let's explore four passages from the book of Psalms explaining why we have difficulty trusting God.

- **Psalm 20:7-8:** "Some trust in chariots, and some in horses; but we will remember the name of the LORD our God. They have bowed down and fallen; but we have risen and stand upright."

  At times we all feel helpless, so we desire some kind of control. Sometimes we don't trust God. It seems easier to trust in human power because it is visible. We become obsessed with money, assets or whatever we think gives us power. It is not wrong to have money or to own property or to have authority, but these things can't become substitutes for trusting in God.

- **Psalm 31:14-19:** "But as for me, I trust in You, O LORD; I say, 'You are my God.' My times are in Your hand; deliver me from the hand of my enemies, and from those who persecute me. Make Your face shine upon Your servant; save me for Your mercies' sake. Do not let me be ashamed, O LORD, for I have called upon You; let the wicked be ashamed; let them be silent in the grave. Let the lying lips be put to silence, which speak insolent things proudly and contemptuously against the righteous. Oh, how great is

Your goodness, which You have laid up for those who fear You, which You have prepared for those who trust in You in the presence of the sons of men!"

Sometimes we don't really trust in God's goodness. We don't believe that he will work in our lives for the good. We don't trust that he has our best interests at heart. When we have that level of distrust in God, it is impossible to have any willingness to trust in imperfect human beings.

- **Psalm 37:1-8:** In this passage David shows three ways we can lose trust in God.

  Verses 1-2: By envying those who have money or fame, or seem to have "perfect" lives.

  Verses 3-6: By not committing our ways to Him in obedience.

  Verses 7-8: By not letting go of our anxiety and anger, and thereby learning to "rest in the LORD."

- **Psalm 40:1-4:** "I waited patiently for the LORD; And He inclined to me, and heard my cry. He also brought me up out of a horrible pit, out of the miry clay, and set my feet upon a rock, and established my steps. He has put a new song in my mouth—Praise to our God; many will see it and fear, and will trust in the LORD. Blessed is that man who makes the LORD his trust, and does not respect the proud, nor such as turn aside to lies."

  The key to David's deliverance was that he "waited patiently" for God. Here is a great difficulty for human beings—to trust the unseen God when we have to wait for his answer.

Let's be honest—all of us at times suffer from not fully trusting God.

Every time we live by the wrong values of society in order to fit in, or allow ourselves to be overcome with anxiety and fear, or engage in constant conflict with others, we're telling God, "I don't trust you. I don't have confidence in your honesty, reliability, integrity and goodness."

And this brings us to a great human dilemma—if we don't trust God, whom do we trust? What keeps us from ultimately trusting God? We must face the harsh reality that we don't trust God because we trust ourselves more. This is a result of feeling and thinking like a spiritual orphan instead of like a child of God.

Study the biblical promises God makes to those who trust him. Go to God and ask him to fulfill those promises, and then step out on faith that he will do what he says. Trusting in God's honesty, reliability, integrity and goodness is the only answer to the orphan spirit that causes us to trust only ourselves.

## Rebuilding Trust with Other People

The reason we find it hard to trust other people is that no human being's behavior is 100 percent consistent. Sometimes even the best of us can be harsh or uncaring, and all of us have experienced being betrayed or terribly hurt by the mean-spirited actions, or simply unthinking actions, of other people whom we trusted.

It's easy to fall into an attitude of "I'm not going to trust anyone." This is a way of saying "I'm going to trust only myself." It is impossible to have healthy, loving relationships without trust.

Someone will say, "But if I trust I'll get hurt." Yes, you will. But remember, every person who chooses to trust you will also experience some hurt because of you. This doesn't mean that you should trust untrustworthy people, but it does mean that we must choose to trust others knowing that no one's behavior is 100 percent consistent.

How can we know when to trust and when not to trust?

Trust is ultimately based on actions, but it also involves intent. We can better understand a person's actions by finding out his or her intent. In *The Speed of Trust*, Covey makes these points about intent:

- Intent matters.

- It grows out of character.

- While we tend to judge ourselves by our intent, we tend to judge others by their behavior.

- We also tend to judge others' intent based on our own paradigms and experience.

- Our perception of intent has a huge impact on trust.

- People often distrust us because of the conclusions they draw about what we do.

- It is important for us to strive to influence the conclusions others draw by 'declaring our intent' (Free Press, 2006, p. 76).

This last point is vital in creating trust. This means that to build trust you must communicate your intentions and work hard to have your behavior match those intentions. The more your behavior is consistent with your stated intentions the more people will trust you and the easier it is for them to forgive you when you fail.

> **Example:** You tell your children that dinner time is important family time. You support your stated intent by consistently showing up for family dinner. Over time, because you have built trust, family members will accept your explanation on those occasions when you can't make it. When you tell them that you are sorry they are quick to forgive because they see the consistency of your behavior.

On the other hand, if you tell them that family meals are important, but you miss three or four dinners every week and you keep saying, "I'll make it up to you," they will eventually distrust you and resent you because your behavior didn't match your stated intentions. Buying gifts to cover up your inconsistent behavior will only cause them to trust you even less.

Another difficulty we face is that we tend to judge others by our own experiences and emotions. How many times do we make a judgment about someone based on our own experiences and without getting all of the facts? We automatically distrust so we automatically impute evil motives.

**Example:** A woman doesn't like beards on men. In front of her daughter she regularly complains about any man with a beard. She says things like, "What is he trying to hide? or "I can't trust a man who covers his face." Her daughter grows up with that as her paradigm. Years later the daughter sees a news report of a crime and the suspect has a beard. Without any knowledge of the crime or the suspect she automatically feels he is guilty.

Sometimes we will even judge another person's intention by superimposing our own intentions upon that individual's actions.

Behavior is important. God judges our behavior. If a person's behavior is consistently untrustworthy, then he can't be trusted. However, you must also be careful about distrusting others because you have prejudged them based on subjective misconceptions.

We will never find peace with God until we replace our orphan spirit with a spirit of trust and confidence in Him. Only then can we experience healthy, loving and trusting relationships with others.

Remember, trusting others is difficult because no one's behavior is 100 percent consistent—and neither is yours. Everyone who chooses to open his or her heart to trust another person will experience some pain. The alternative is to go through life bitter and alone, but this is not the life God wants for us. It all comes down to the simplest of concepts taught by Jesus Christ. We must love God with all of our hearts, souls and minds, and we must love our neighbor as ourselves. We can never experience this love until we first have the courage to trust.

## Forgiveness-Repentance-Relationship

A key to conflict management is to remember that all of us have been offended and all of us have offended. We've all been on both sides of the equation. This knowledge can keep us humble and focused no matter which side of the equation on which we find ourselves.

A greater issue arises when a person who has done a grievous wrong refuses to repent. Through the years I've talked with many people who were abused as children. Sometimes when a parent who abused an individual faces death, the abused person wants to reconnect somehow, seeking the parent's repentance and consequent closure. But what if the abuser refuses to acknowledge the wrong or even blames the person who was abused as the culprit?

The Bible instructs victims of injustice to give up the need for vengeance. We must be forgiving in order not to spend the rest of our lives in turmoil and anger. On the other hand, continuing in a relationship with the abuser is contingent upon his or her repentance.

Remember God's example. He offers us forgiveness while we are still his enemies, but a relationship with him requires our repentance. It is the same spiritual application in human relationships. We are to seek God's peace in us and offer forgiveness to those who have abused us. This means giving up allowing the other person to control our thoughts and emotions. It also means being willing to pay the price of reconciliation by praying for the person and being available to rebuild the relationship. Even if the offender doesn't repent, the person who was offended is now able to experience peace.

Let's next look at why you may be struggling with being reconciled to God.

# 7

# The Conflict Within

If the solution to human conflict is first to be reconciled to God, why is that so difficult?

As a pastor, I've sat with many people who struggle with accepting God's forgiveness. Do you? Have you ever thought, "I messed up again; God can't forgive me"?

Being reconciled to God involves not only accepting Christ's sacrifice for your sins, but also participating in a process the Bible calls *repentance*.

I remember a conversation I had with a woman years ago about Israel's King David. She had lived a good life by anyone's standards. She had never robbed a convenience store, committed adultery or killed anyone. She was upset because she thought God was unfair in how he, in her viewpoint, let David off the hook for his terrible sins.

How can we reconcile David's sins with him being honored throughout the Bible as a man of God? This question is important when we face those times when we fail miserably as Christians and then wonder how to return to God.

David's headlong fall into sin, and his remarkable response to God recorded in Psalm 51, is a moving example of God's mercy and the human response of real repentance. This is a lesson the woman who thought God had cut David too much slack needed to learn.

In David's story we find encouragement in seeing that no matter how atrocious our sins, God is willing to show mercy. His arms are open in forgiveness, but reconciliation requires us to be willing to repent.

Our narrative begins more than 3,000 years ago on a warm night in Jerusalem. King David couldn't sleep. The affairs of state weighed heavily on his mind; his army was campaigning against the people of Ammon. As he paced the palace's roof top patio, something caught his eye. On the roof of a nearby house a beautiful woman was taking a bath.

David had a choice. He could have turned and walked away. Instead, he watched. Eventually, he called some of his servants and told them to bring the woman to the palace. She was Bathsheba, the wife of a Hittite soldier named Uriah who was serving in David's army. The biblical story would lead us to believe that Uriah had converted to the worship of the God of Israel. He is listed as one of David's "mighty men" who were famous for their courage and personal loyalty to the king.

When the servants brought Uriah's wife to the palace, he sexually forced himself upon her. The result was that she became pregnant.

The king now plotted to cover up his sin. He called Uriah back from the front lines of battle, had him give a report and sent him home to be with his wife. The plan failed when Uriah refused to be with his wife while his comrades were still at the front. Uriah was an honorable man.

David was faced with another choice. He could confess his sins before God and tell Uriah the truth. Unwilling to reconcile with God, and driven by fear and anxiety that Uriah would discover the adulterous affair, David planned to rectify the situation deceitfully.

He sent a written message with Uriah to give to Joab, who was the army's commander. The message instructed Joab to put Uriah in the most dangerous part of the battle and then to retreat from him so that he would be killed. Unknowingly, Uriah delivered his own death warrant to his commander. This loyal soldier died in battle while defending his country, having been betrayed by his king.

David tried to carry on with life as though nothing had happened. God finally confronted him through the prophet Nathan.

Nathan approached the king and asked for a ruling on a theft that had taken place. The prophet told of a rich man and poor man who lived next to each other. The poor man had one little lamb that was a family pet. The rich man possessed huge flocks of sheep and herds of cattle. A traveler came to visit the rich man, and instead of the rich man killing one of his own animals for a meal, he stole the poor man's pet lamb, serving it to his guest.

David was incensed. He declared, "As the LORD lives, the man who has done this shall surely die! And he shall restore fourfold for the lamb, because he did this thing and because he had no pity."

In response, Nathan told David "YOU are the man!"

Imagine the unbearable silence as David is filled with anxiety, guilt and fear. His sins had found him out. Nathan wasn't finished. God had a message for the king:

> "'I anointed you king over Israel, and I delivered you from the hand of Saul. I gave you your master's house and your master's wives into your keeping, and gave you the house of Israel and Judah. And if that had been too little, I also would have given you much more! Why have you despised the commandment of the LORD, to do evil in His sight? You have killed Uriah the Hittite with

the sword; you have taken his wife to be your wife, and have killed him with the sword of the people of Ammon. Now therefore, the sword shall never depart from your house, because you have despised Me, and have taken the wife of Uriah the Hittite to be your wife.' Thus says the LORD: 'Behold, I will raise up adversity against you from your own house; and I will take your wives before your eyes and give them to your neighbor, and he shall lie with your wives in the sight of this sun. For you did it secretly, but I will do this thing before all Israel, before the sun'" (2 Samuel 12:7-12).

God's judgment on David was severe. Because of David's sins his family would be continually plagued with violence.

Once again, David had a choice. He could claim that his sins weren't his fault. It was Bathsheba's fault for tempting him. It was the stress of being king. He could even claim it was God's fault for not intervening to help him or that God was being too harsh in his punishment.

He simply said to Nathan, "I have sinned against the Lord."

There were no excuses, no blame placed on others, no defense—only the acknowledgment of the depravity of his actions; actions he could not take back.

Nathan then said to David, "The Lord also has put away your sin; you shall not die. However, because by this deed you have given great occasion to the enemies of the Lord to blaspheme, the child also who is born to you shall surely die" (2 Samuel 12:13-14).

Through God's forgiveness, and David's repentance, the king was reconciled to God. God would not require his death for his crimes. But God's forgiveness did not erase the immediate consequences of sin. Because David's sin was public, God would exact a public penalty—the child born from the king's sin would die. Everyone would know of David's sins and God's judgment upon him.

You may look at David's story and think, "God's going to punish me anyway, so why try?"

The fact that David would suffer because of his sins isn't the end of the story.

## What is Missing?

So here you and I sit. Many individuals have addictions to pornography, or guilt because they know they drink too much, or nagging anxiety about showing up at church once a week but ignoring God with selfish, dishonest lifestyles the rest of the week. And of course there is all of the conflict in our lives—the broken families, the anger and the hurt. Sin, in action or thought, creates a barrier between us and God. Only God can tear down that barrier.

King David's life changed dramatically as he faced his sins and turned to God. Even if you are suffering the devastating consequences of sins—experiencing a broken marriage, being a slave to anger, or feeling cut off from God—God can change your life in a dramatic, wonderful way. God can heal you when you open your heart and mind to real repentance.

The profound lesson from the story of King David is that he truly repented and experienced God's forgiveness.

David was a poet and songwriter. He put his expression of repentance into words and music. We read of David's repentance in Psalm 51. In it we have one man's experience of repentance, and through his experience, an example of how to return to God when we have been separated by our sins.

We know the occasion for this Psalm in the heading: "To the Chief Musician. A Psalm of David when Nathan the prophet went to him, after he had gone in to Bathsheba." David's Psalm is filled with heartfelt words as he seeks not just relief from the consequences of his sins, but a restored relationship with God. He wrote,

"Have mercy upon me, O God, according to Your lovingkindness; according to the multitude of Your tender mercies, blot out my transgressions. Wash me thoroughly from my iniquity, and cleanse me from my sin. For I acknowledge my transgressions, and my sin is always before me. Against You, You only, have I sinned, and done this evil in Your sight—that You may be found just when You speak, and blameless when You judge" (Psalm 51:1-4).

At the heart of David's repentance is the understanding that all sin is against God. David understood that God determines right and wrong. Sin damages your relationship with the sinless God. David confronted his sin. He even hated it. There is no true repentance without taking responsibility for and despising your sins. David also understood God's capacity for mercy. God wants to forgive you so that your relationship with him can be restored.

David uses three words to describe his spiritual state. These Hebrew words are translated into English as:

- *"transgressions"*—The Hebrew word he used *"Signifies willful deviation from, and therefore rebellion against, the path of godly living."*

- *"iniquity"*—*"An offense, intentionally or not, against God's law."*

- *"sin"*—The word David uses here isn't the usual Hebrew word for sin, but a word that primarily means *"missing the mark or the path."*

(*Vine's Expository Dictionary of Biblical Words*, Thomas Nelson Publishers, 1985)

David doesn't give excuses for sinning. He simply asks God to "wash me." He doesn't want a superficial sprinkling—he wants his mind and heart scrubbed. He asks God to "blot out" his sins. This term is powerful in its ancient context—ancient paper wasn't as porous as modern paper and ink wasn't as easily absorbed. A writer, using the right compound, could blot paper and erase the ink completely.

Continuing from verse 6:

> "Behold, You desire truth in the inward parts, and in the hidden part You will make me to know wisdom. Purge me with hyssop, and I shall be clean; wash me, and I shall be whiter than snow. Make me hear joy and gladness, that the bones You have broken may rejoice. Hide Your face from my sins, and blot out all my iniquities" (Psalm 51:6-9).

David was concerned with more than just a few changes in behavior. He understood that God wants "truth in the inward parts."

You can possess great biblical knowledge, and even practice what most people would consider a religious life, but if your mind is filled with envy, self-righteousness, anger, unwillingness to forgive, hatred and sexual lust, then you have to ask yourself whether you are you seeking "truth in the inward parts."

You and I can hide our "inward parts" by appearing religious. God wants to rip open our minds and hearts to expose all of the corruption of our "inward parts" and to replace our lawlessness with truth. This isn't something you and I can do on our own. Only God can heal our damaged minds and hearts.

There are hidden sins that keep us from accepting God's power in our lives. David tried to hide his "inward parts" by going on with daily life as if nothing had happened after he had taken Bathsheba and murdered her husband. When Nathan confronted him with his sins, David had a choice to hide his "inward parts" or to expose them to the light of God.

Much of the time we live our lives out of touch with our own motivations. Our emotions and thoughts are nothing more than responses to what is happening around us. It's only when we take time to reflect on God's ways, his laws and his mercy, and then to confess our sins, that we can experience what it really means to be forgiven. Only then can we experience the "joy and gladness" that David expressed in his psalm.

Next David wrote,

"Create in me a clean heart, O God, and renew a steadfast spirit within me. Do not cast me away from Your presence, and do not take Your Holy Spirit from me" (Psalm 51:10-11).

David asked God to create in him a "clean heart." The heart refers to the mind, the will and the center of a person's thoughts and emotions. David understood that his outward sins were products of his inner self.

Are you prepared to go before God and to ask for a clean heart? Not just for his forgiveness, but for a change of heart and mind? It's easy to want God's forgiveness, to want him to take away the painful consequences of sin, but desiring a "clean heart" is more than just wanting to be forgiven. It is a desire to be reconciled to him in a submissive, humble and childlike relationship.

David showed why he is called a man after God's own heart. He wanted everything about him to be pleasing to God—his behavior, his motivations, his thoughts and his emotions. He wanted to be a "kindred spirit" with God.

The psalmist continued:

"Restore to me the joy of Your salvation, and uphold me by Your generous Spirit. Then I will teach transgressors Your ways, and sinners shall be converted to You" (Psalm 51:12-13).

David knew real peace and joy can come only from a restored relationship with God. He recognized that God's forgiveness was a precious and powerful gift. Once David was restored to the "joy of salvation," he was motivated to tell others about repentance and restoration.

## Grace in the Old Testament?

There is a misconception among many Christians that the Old Testament is strictly a book about law and the New Testament deals exclusively with grace. Jesus, in the Sermon on the Mount, said that there would be those who profess his name but are rejected by him because they "practice lawlessness." In Romans the apostle Paul said that he wouldn't know the definition of sin without the law. There is plenty of law in the New Testament.

Here in the Old Testament passage of Psalm 51 we find one of the most intense personal expressions of a man who experienced God's grace. He knew he couldn't earn God's forgiveness. David was trapped in the awful reality of his crimes against God and his fellow man. If God didn't give him divine favor, or grace, then his life was void of meaning except to suffer and die.

David understood that what God wanted from him was the sacrifice of a "broken spirit":

> "Deliver me from the guilt of bloodshed, O God, the God
> of my salvation, and my tongue shall sing aloud of Your
> righteousness. O Lord, open my lips, and my mouth shall
> show forth Your praise. For You do not desire sacrifice, or
> else I would give it; You do not delight in burnt offering.
> The sacrifices of God are a broken spirit, a broken and
> a contrite heart—these, O God, You will not despise"
> (Psalm 51:14-17).

What does it mean to have a broken spirit and contrite heart before God? Our spirit and heart get damaged by sin. That's why we are filled with anxiety, depression, feelings of inferiority and anger. That is why we resist God's forgiveness. To experience reconciliation with God, we must confront our hardened, arrogant and selfish nature.

As our Father, God wants us to be broken before him. He wants us to be like David, taking responsibility for our depraved and sinful nature. He wants us to come before him humbly, desperately aware of our need for him, desperately in need of his grace. Notice the sincerity and desperation of Psalm 51. David is consumed with the awareness of his need for God's mercy and love.

It is normal for human beings to reject the approach to God exemplified by David in Psalm 51. Too many times we approach God only when we need help. Too often we want to deny or justify our sins. We believe that we have the right to harbor anger, hatred, jealousy, envy and arrogance. We want to use God's grace as a license to sin.

There is a need in the half-hearted, secularized Christian world to practice true repentance and to be reconciled to God. The power of David's psalm reaches across the centuries. Now is the time to get on your knees, to ask God for a clean heart, to ask your Creator for truth in the inward parts, and to ask your Father for a broken and contrite spirit.

A broken spirit means just that—to be broken and humbled before God. You may not like what you see revealed by truth in your inward parts. Repentance is a painful realization of your absolute spiritual poverty before God and your need for his grace.

Only through God's forgiveness and your response of repentance can you experience true freedom from the shackles of sin, be reconciled to God and have the power to overcome habits and addictions. Only then will you begin to resolve the conflicts in your life.

God sent his Son to die as the substitute for punishment you and I deserve. This is the ultimate expression of God's grace, his favor, his pardon and his cleansing that give us spiritual healing that we can't provide for ourselves.

# 8

# The Peacemaker: Standing in the Gap

Everyone knew Abigail's marriage was a bad match. Her husband might be wealthy, but there is nothing more despicable than a mean-spirited man who uses his wealth to take advantage of the less fortunate. Even his name, Nabal, meant "fool." Abigail, a woman of intelligence and beauty, would surely wilt from living in such a harsh relationship.

It was a time of political unrest for Israel. Rumor was that King Saul was becoming irrational since his rejection by the great prophet Samuel. Then there was this young upstart named David, a shepherd from an unknown family, who had killed Goliath. Saul, intent on doing David harm, had driven him from Jerusalem. The young claimant to the throne was now roaming the countryside with a band of loyal troops protecting herders from marauders.

Nabal's flocks were under the protection of David's small army of six hundred soldiers. The wealthy rancher was in the field shearing sheep when David's messengers arrived, reminding Nabal of the protection afforded his flocks. Explaining that they were low on food, the messengers asked the wealthy rancher to send some supplies. True to form, Nabal refused, claiming David was nothing more than a runaway slave.

When the messengers told David, he was outraged. He gathered four hundred of his troops to march on Nabal's residence to settle the matter.

Abigail was startled by the fear on the face of the young servant who begged to speak to her. He informed her about the way David's men had protected the flocks, and he explained how messengers had come to Nabal asking for food, but were treated rudely. It wouldn't be long before David's men arrived to seek justice. Nabal was so stubborn he wouldn't listen to anyone.

Abigail quickly decided what she must do. She had servants load donkeys with two hundred loaves of bread, wine, mutton, roasted grain, raisins and figs. There was no use in telling Nabal since he would restrain her from going. Instead, she led her small caravan to intercept David's approaching warriors. Abigail knew she was taking her life in her own hands.

Abigail approached David and bowed before him. She had in her grasp the opportunity to escape a less than happy marriage. Surely no one who knew her husband would blame Abigail if she asked David to spare her and the servants, punishing only Nabal. What she actually said is quite remarkable:

> "On me, my lord, on me let this iniquity be! And please let your maidservant speak in your ears, and hear the words of your maidservant.
>
> Please, let not my lord regard this scoundrel Nabal. For as his name is, so is he: Nabal is his name, and folly is with him. But I, your maidservant, did not see the young men of my lord whom you sent.
>
> Now therefore, my lord, as the LORD lives and as your soul lives, since the LORD has held you back from coming to bloodshed and from avenging yourself with your own hand, now then, let your enemies and those who seek harm for my lord be as Nabal.

And now this present which your maidservant has brought to my lord, let it be given to the young men who follow my lord.

Please forgive the trespass of your maidservant. For the LORD will certainly make for my lord an enduring house, because my lord fights the battles of the LORD, and evil is not found in you throughout your days.

Yet a man has risen to pursue you and seek your life, but the life of my lord shall be bound in the bundle of the living with the LORD your God; and the lives of your enemies He shall sling out, as from the pocket of a sling.

And it shall come to pass, when the LORD has done for my lord according to all the good that He has spoken concerning you, and has appointed you ruler over Israel, that this will be no grief to you, nor offense of heart to my lord, either that you have shed blood without cause, or that my lord has avenged himself. But when the LORD has dealt well with my lord, then remember your maidservant" (1 Samuel 25:24-31).

The silence seemed to last hours as everyone waited for David's response. Instead of pleading for her own life, Abigail interceded for her cantankerous husband. The next few minutes would decide her fate.

Finally, David spoke:

"Blessed is the LORD God of Israel, who sent you this day to meet me! And blessed is your advice and blessed are you, because you have kept me this day from coming to bloodshed and from avenging myself with my own hand. For indeed, as the LORD God of Israel lives, who has kept me back from hurting you, unless you had hastened and come to meet me, surely by morning light no males would have been left to Nabal!" (1 Samuel 25:32-34).

Abigail returned home to find Nabal in a drunken stupor. She decided to wait until morning to tell him of her meeting with David. The next morning a hung-over Nabal listened in deepening terror as his wife told him of how narrowly he had missed being killed because of his stubborn rudeness. He collapsed into a coma never to regain consciousness. Ten days later Nabal died.

Abigail had every reason to blame Nabal for being a lousy husband. She could have used David's anger as a means to free herself from an unhappy marriage. Instead, her decision was based on doing what was right, regardless of her personal feelings. Abigail's reaction to the situation stems from who she was, not from who Nabal was.

This is one of the great secrets of conflict resolution. Biblical principles must trump emotions. Your reactions must come from your concepts of right and wrong, not from the wrong actions or words of the other person.

Abigail is an example of a person who rose above her unhappy marriage because she based her responses on righteous principles of right and wrong, not on her emotional reactions to a selfish husband. She influenced David. As a result, rather than reacting emotionally to Nabal's rudeness, David's response was based on the ethical principles God expected from him. There is an interesting twist to Abigail's story. When David heard of Nabal's death, once again he sent messengers to his house, only this time to ask for Abigail's hand in marriage.

## Peacemaking and Intercession

When people found out that Jesus was in a nearby house, they flocked to the place until every room was crammed with folks wanting to see the preacher who performed healings. Four men carried a paralytic to Jesus, hoping for a miracle. The four men couldn't get their friend through the crowd. Desperately, they climbed onto the roof, ripped it open, and lowered the paralyzed man into the house. Jesus rewarded their faith by healing the man (Mark 2:1-12).

In this story we find a remarkable example of intercession. Intercession is the act of pleading or praying on behalf of another person. The four men took extraordinary actions to help their incapacitated friend get to Jesus. Christians who face illness or life's difficulties often ask other Christians to pray for them. When suffering, we find it comforting to know that someone else is going to God on our behalf.

The book of Hebrews describes how Israel's high priest offered intercessory sacrifices for the sins of the people. The writer explains that these sacrifices were symbolic of the reality of Jesus Christ as our great intercessor. Christ stands in the gap between the holy God and corrupt human beings, pleading on our behalf (Hebrews 7-10; note 7:25).

Paul wrote to the church in Rome, "It is Christ who died, and furthermore is also risen, who is even at the right hand of God, who also makes intercession for us" (Romans 8:34).

When you pray, you are led directly into the presence of God through the intercession of Christ. It's easy to follow Christ's example by interceding for a friend who is suffering, but Christ also interceded for individuals who sinned against him. How is a Christian supposed to intercede in relationship with a person who has personally sinned against him or her?

When Moses was on Mount Sinai receiving the Ten Commandments from God, the people of Israel returned to the pagan customs of Egypt. A couple of months earlier God had destroyed the greatest economic and military power on earth though 10 terrible plagues. He had opened the Red Sea so the

Israelites could cross on dry land. They now camped below a mountain where God's presence was visible in a fiery cloud, yet they rejected him. God's justice for this rebellion required the destruction of the people. Moses pleaded to God on their behalf (Exodus 32:1-14).

The Psalmist describes these events:

> "They made a golden calf in Horeb, and worshipped the molded image. Thus they changed their glory into the image of an ox that eats grass. They forgot God their Savior, who had done great things in Egypt, wondrous works in the land of Ham, awesome things by the Red Sea. Therefore He said that He would destroy them, had not Moses His chosen one stood before Him in the breach, to turn away His wrath, lest He destroy them" (Psalm 106:19-23).

This account doesn't present us with an out-of-control, angry God who changed his mind because he is calmed down by Moses. The Bible reveals that God acts consistently with his character. He becomes angry because of human rebellion and sin. This is consistent with his goodness and justice. He is also quick to forgive and offer reconciliation if the person repents. This is consistent with his love.

It is also consistent with his character that he will allow individuals to intercede for others. Moses carried out the role of intercessor by pleading to God for the people of Israel, who were still sinning and had not yet come to repentance.

During the time of Samuel, the last judge of Israel, the people demanded a king so their government would be like other nations. They soon began to realize that their rejection of Samuel was, in effect, a rejection of God, who had ordained him to be their judge. They approached Samuel and said, "Pray for your servants to the LORD your God, that we may not die." Samuel replied, "far be it from me that I should sin against the LORD in ceasing to pray for you; but I will teach you the good and the right way" (1 Samuel 12:19, 23).

In the cases of Moses and Samuel, we find men of God who interceded for people when they had sinned.

The ultimate expression of intercession is Christ, who died as a substitute sacrifice for us and now acts as the intercessor between us and God. Jesus expands this principle to praying for those who sin against you personally. In the Sermon on the Mount he said,

> "You have heard that is was said, 'You shall love your neighbor and hate your enemy.' But I say to you, love your enemies, bless those who curse you, do good to those who hate you, and pray for those who spitefully use you and persecute you, that you may be sons of your Father in heaven; for He makes His sun rise on the evil and on the good, and sends rain on the just and on the unjust" (Matthew 5:43-45).

Intercessory prayer can't magically reconcile another person to God. Everyone is personally responsible for repentance, but intercessory prayer can put you on the same page as God. God may even use you as an instrument to help bring a person to repentance, or help someone who is distraught. In God's plan you may be instrumental in bringing your enemy into peace with God.

"Blessed are the peacemakers, for they shall be called the sons of God" (Matthew 5:9).

This book is a starting point on the Christian journey of being forgiven by God, forgiving others and learning how to manage conflict. Remember what I wrote in the preface—authentic

Christianity isn't a "you have finally arrived" experience. The conviction to be a true disciple of Jesus Christ is a daily adventure of ever learning and ever changing by applying the teachings of the Master.

Made in the USA
Monee, IL
10 September 2020